Bible Study Series

Jonah, Esther, and Ruth

Servants of Deliverance and Grace

Marie Coody

Jeannie McCullough, Executive Editor

ISBN 083-411-979X

Cover Design: Darlene Filley

Library of Congress Cataloging-in-Publication Data

Coody, Marie, 1925-
Jonah, Esther, and Ruth : servants of deliverance and grace / Marie Coody.
p. cm. — (Wisdom of the Word Bible study series)
Includes bibliographical references.
ISBN 0-8341-1979-X (pbk.)
1. Bible. O.T. Jonah—Criticism, interpretation, etc. 2. Bible. O.T. Esther—Criticism, interpretation, etc. 3. Bible. O.T. Ruth—Criticism, interpretation, etc. 4. Bible—Study. I. Title. II. Series.
BS1605.5 .C66 2002
221'.35'0071—dc21

2002009219

10 9 8 7 6 5 4 3 2 1

Contents

About Wisdom of the Word

Wisdom of the Word (W.O.W.) was founded in 1986 by Jeannie McCullough in Bethany, Oklahoma. It began as a weekly Bible study at Bethany First Church of the Nazarene. In the first year the study grew to over 400 members, and women from other churches and the community began joining. The local enrollment of Wisdom of the Word eventually exceeded 1,000 and has included men, women, and children of all ages and many denominations. Wisdom of the Word has been an instrument in uniting the community of believers as well as reaching the unchurched and the lost. It is now ministering to thousands through videos and cassette tapes and other programs such as Children of the Word, prison ministries, and missions.

About the Name

W.O.W. began as "Women of the Word." Then when men began to join in the study with the women, the name was changed to Wisdom of the Word, not only to retain the W.O.W. acronym but also to reflect the mission:

> To have our lives visibly changed by gaining wisdom from God's Word and responding in radical obedience to His voice.

About Jeannie McCullough

Jeannie McCullough is a pastor's wife, mother, and grandmother. Her life and ministry have taken her to Bethany, Oklahoma, where her husband, Mel, is the senior pastor at Bethany First Church of the Nazarene. She understands firsthand how radical obedience to God's Word can change a life.

Southern Nazarene University granted Jeannie an honorary doctorate in 1997. Due to her humor and honesty as well as her unique insights and application of the Scriptures in daily living, she is in great demand as a speaker throughout North America. Jeannie strives to be a "salt tablet" who will make others thirsty for God's Word. As she has committed herself to being a student of the Word, God has given her many opportunities to share what He is teaching her.

About the Author

Marie Coody's lifelong commitment to know God and His Word has led her to study His Scriptures and given her the opportunity to serve her church in many areas and teach almost every age.

While mentoring young mothers who became partners with Jeannie McCullough in creating Wisdom of the Word Bible study, Marie became a member of the Wisdom of the Word board. Her continuing in-depth study of the Bible led her into writing Bible lessons with applications from His Word into everyday lives.

Marie and her husband, Darwyn, enjoy spending time with their daughters, Lyn and Marcia, and Marcia's husband, George.

Interested in starting a W.O.W. Bible study?

If you are interested in starting a W.O.W. Bible study, attending a study in your area, or ordering additional materials, please contact the W.O.W. outreach office in Bethany, Oklahoma, at 405-491-6274.

Introduction to Jonah

Although the Book of Jonah consists of only four chapters with 48 verses and can be read in 10 minutes or less, the lessons in it impact the reader quickly and profoundly. It is a historical narrative full of dramatic, action-packed events that tell the story of the prophet instead of emphasizing his prophecies. The main character is neither Jonah nor the great fish, but God, who is mentioned 38 times.

Jonah was a resident of Gath Hepher, located in Zebulon territory, now known as Galilee. He was the son of Amattia and ministered as a true prophet of the Lord in the Northern Kingdom during the reign of Jeroboam II, about 786-746 B.C.

Among the books of the 12 minor prophets, 11 of them contain primarily the messages delivered to their people. In the Book of Jonah, the only recorded preaching of the prophet is eight words to the most important city in the Gentile nation of Assyria: "Forty more days and Nineveh will be overturned" (3:4). The other 11 prophetic books give few references of personal history of the prophets, while the Book of Jonah, in all four chapters, gives descriptions of events in Jonah's life.

In all other books of the prophets, men proclaimed faithfully the judgment of God, which turns people to repentance; but Jonah was unwilling to proclaim God's judgment upon the people of Nineveh because of his fear that they might repent and therefore be saved from destruction.

During the life of Jonah, Assyria was in a period of decline. Three consecutive weak kings had resulted in lowering its prestige and power on the world scene. Babylon, however, was becoming a stronger power to be considered. The people were feeling uncertain and insecure about the future of Assyria. God chose this time for His Spirit to move upon Nineveh and had chosen Jonah to be His messenger to the lost Ninevites. Many of Jonah's countrymen had experienced barbaric atrocities from the fierce Assyrians. Never would Jonah want to be on a missionary trip anywhere in Assyria and especially to its largest city, Nineveh. So he headed in the opposite direction—but he could not run from God.

"Red and yellow, black and white, they are precious in His sight" is a message that speaks to us "as we watch Jonah—narrow, vindictive, nationalistic, bitterly exclusive—clutching his faith to his bosom while God seeks to get him to share it in His broader purpose of redemption."[1]

As you begin each day, use this acrostic to help you study:

***W**ait for the Holy Spirit to teach you as you read His Word.*

***O**bey what God instructs you to do.*

***R**emember to praise God for insights and promises fulfilled.*

***D**iscover for yourself the incredible faithfulness of God!*

Bible Study Series

Jonah

LESSON 1

■ **A study of Jonah 1—2:9**

DAY ONE

Believers Hear God

Read Jonah 1, concentrating on verse 1.

1. *The word of the* L*ORD came to* _____________ _____________ *of Amittai.*

We want to be able to say, "The word of the Lord came to _____________ child of _____________."
[your name] [name of your mother or father]

2. Record only the phrase (four or five words) describing how each of the following men were given God's call to become a prophet.

   Isaiah 6:8

   Jeremiah 1:4-5

   Amos 7:15

For different reasons each of these prophets, like Jonah, did not immediately say yes to God, but in their obedience to Him they accepted His call.

3. According to 1 John 1:3, with whom are we to have fellowship?

4. Record our call from God in 1 Corinthians 1:9.

Fellowship is defined as companionship—sharing together. God wants companionship with us. He wants to share life with us.

5. From 1 John 1:6 explain what keeps us from fellowship with Him.

6. From 1 John 1:7 explain how we are equipped for fellowship with God and other believers.

7. From the following verses explain how we can know that God lives in us.

   1 John 3:24

MEMORY CHALLENGE

Ezekiel 18:21

If a wicked man turns away from the sins he has committed and keeps all my decrees and does what is just and right, he will surely live; he will not die.

1 John 4:12

1 John 4:13

1 John 4:15

8. Record what John 8:47 explains about hearing God.

We belong to God, and we want to hear Him.

In Matthew 11:15 and in 14 other places in the New Testament, Jesus makes the statement *He who has ears, let him hear.* Isn't He saying to us, "You who have spiritual ears choose to use them to hear spiritual truth"? Without this choice, communion in prayer, meditation in His Word, and hearing from Him are not possible. Once we have chosen to hear Him, the ability to hear Him must be developed. Until hearing God becomes a priority to us, we will not learn quickly or correctly to discern His voice. As we make a deliberate choice and make a determined effort to set our minds on God, the enemy will do anything he can to prevent it—but the Lord will do everything He can to help us. We must dispel the thoughts that Satan and self bring to our mind and replace them with God's truths. In time it will become a spontaneous, natural reflex to immediately turn to God in all circumstances.

We must not let others hear God for us. When we listen to friends, books, sermons, or experts, we may accept or reject what we hear; but when we hear from God himself, our choice is to obey Him, or we will live in disobedience—which is sin.

To hear God we need a pure heart. James 4:8 tells us to come near to God and He in turn will come near to us. We must wash sin out of our lives and purify our hearts. We cannot be double-minded, trying to follow God and the world at the same time. Our hearts must be pure, with a desire to follow God only. As we continue in obedience to His Word, sin will be washed out of our lives and replaced with truth.

As we listen to God and obey Him, we will hear more and more from Him—not because He is speaking more to us, but because we're developing the ability to hear what He's saying to us. By training ourselves to ignore the distractions of the world, we become less aware of them and more aware of Him.

Have you had a call on your life that gave your whole life new direction? As His children, we can't escape the pressure of the mind of God on our minds. His call does not come from any other person. It is discerned through the Holy Spirit from His mind to our hearts and minds. We know the truth of Jesus' words in John 3:8—*The wind blows wherever it pleases. You hear its sound, but you cannot tell where it comes from or where it is going. So it is with everyone born of the Spirit.*

The word of the Lord came to Amos, a simple herdsman, as he tended his flock. It came to Isaiah while he was praying in the Temple. It came to Jeremiah when he was only a child. It came to Jonah, and he didn't want to obey.

Paul explains in Acts 17:26-28 that from Adam God made every person in the entire world. He decides when we will live on the earth and the exact places where we will live. God did this so we would seek Him and find Him, although He is always near to each of us. It is in God that we live and move and exist. We are His offspring.

As His children we sense through the Holy Spirit the pressure of His mind on our hearts and minds. It is the pressure of His mind, or the voice of His Holy Spirit, that's the source of all our seeking after good and Him. We've all had our "God moments," when we feel the tug of His Spirit affirming His presence and giving us warning, assurance, answers, and guidance.

Jonah had his "moment." His bitter prejudices and old thought patterns of hostility against the Assyrians swept through his mind, and he decided to run from God's call.

Father, I want to hear You. I want to be of one mind with You. Please show me corrections I need to make in my Christian walk that will allow me to say, "Father, I have spiritual ears—let me hear." I believe You hear me, and I look forward to a closer fellowship with You. I can believe for the answer because Jesus sacrificed himself and made it possible for me.

DAY TWO

Jonah Ran from God

Read Jonah 1:2-3.

1. Why did the Lord ask Jonah to preach against the great city of Nineveh?

2. What was Jonah's response to the Lord's commissioning of him to preach to the Ninevites?

3. From verse 3 list the progression of Jonah's running from God.

4. In your own words explain what Jonah could have learned from the following scriptures.

   Psalm 139:7-12

   Jeremiah 23:23-24

Jonah would have chosen for Nineveh to be destroyed rather than for the city to have an opportunity to repent and be spared. The Assyrians were a cruel people who showed no mercy to their enemies, and Jonah wanted them to come under God's judgment.

Like Jonah, Nahum was a prophet to Nineveh. Secular historical records confirm that the description Nahum gives of Nineveh also describes the city in the time of Jonah.

5. From Nahum 3:1-4, list the characteristics of the Assyrian city of Nineveh:

   Morally

   Spiritually

   Militarily

The atrocities of today's Iraq (ancient Assyria) against the people of Kuwait in 1990-91 reveal to the world that the cruelty of ancient Assyria has been repeated for nearly 3,000 years.

6. Like Jonah, we can be asked to do things in life that we don't want to do. Do you have an experience of running away that you're willing to share with others? Explain what you learned through running away.

Sandra and Karen were so excited to be spending two weeks on the farm. From the last day of school until the day they were to meet each other at Uncle Harlan and Aunt Faye's dairy farm, the fourth graders planned their days together. They would ride horses, swim in the pond, feed the chickens and gather the eggs, give the calves milk from special nursing bottles, bring in vegetables from the garden, play hide-and-seek in the barn with other visiting cousins, and explore the farmland.

Aunt Faye had an agreement with all her visiting nieces that she would prepare all the meals, but she expected them to help by washing the dishes. One evening after enjoying fried chicken, mashed potatoes and gravy, vegetables from the garden, homemade rolls, and peach cobbler, the cousins decided they were having to work too hard in the kitchen. When they complained, they were told they must finish the work they had agreed to do. Aunt Faye wanted them to develop into dependable adults with good work ethics.

After the angry girls had finally completed their tasks, they decided they would leave the farm and walk the two miles to Uncle Weaver and Aunt Ora Dell's farm. Aunt Faye agreed to their plan with the understanding that if they ran away from their problem, they could not return until the following summer. The girls packed their suitcases and left the house. As they walked down the long driveway to the road that would take them to the other farm, they realized it was beginning to get dark. They began having second thoughts about running away from their problem. What could they do now? They couldn't just turn around and go back, admitting they were afraid of the dark. How could they save face with Aunt Faye? They sat down beside the driveway to develop a plan. As it continued getting darker and darker, they began hearing noises (was it mice or snakes?) in the nearby fields.

As the girls sat in the grass, they saw a car approaching and soon they saw the headlights turn into the driveway where they were sitting. It was the aunt and uncle they had planned to visit.

Many years later Aunt Faye confessed that she had watched them from a front window and had called her brother, Weaver, to tell him of the girls' plans.

The following summer the girls again visited the farm for two weeks, agreeing to help with the work and promising not to run away again.

Sandra and Karen were taught a good lesson for life because their aunt had consequences for their running from their responsibilities. Many of us were very young when we began running, withdrawing and isolating ourselves when we were unhappy or hurt by people or circumstances. Like Jonah, we didn't consider how our actions affected others or how we needed to face difficulties and work through them.

Jonah was a reluctant prophet given a mission from God that seemed wrong to him. He hated Nineveh and feared their atrocities. He wanted vengeance, not mercy, for these cruel people. So when he heard God tell him to call the people to repentance, he ran in the opposite direction.

Because God has entrusted us with free will, we're capable of saying yes or no to God. To decide to make God the Lord of our lives and follow His guidance is not as easy as we would like it to be. Initially we may resist, questioning His direction. We're a "Jonah" whenever we resist saying yes to God. We're a "Jonah" as long as we allow bitterness to continue in our hearts toward anyone.

To prepare ourselves for what the Lord may want to say to us, focus on the people you find most difficult to love. On the screen of your consciousness, flash the faces of the persons, the types and groups of people of whom you're the most critical and judgmental. Think of the personalities you write off, hoping never to have contact with or responsibility for them, the person or group who prompts you to say, "If I never see them again, it will be too soon," or "Whatever happens to them, it's less than they deserve!" These are the people who have become enemies in your mind because of what they do, say, or believe. That's what happened to Jonah. He was committed to exclusivity and separatism. There was no room in his prejudiced heart for concern about his enemies.[1]

As we think of Jonah's disobedience, we must decide if we're making a 500-mile trip to Nineveh or traveling 2,000 miles by boat to Tarshish. To proceed to our Nineveh, we're in a place of obedience to those unquestionable revelations of God's commands to us that will involve people, solving problems, facing challenges as well as opportunities. Whatever or whomever our own judgmentalism has declared as an enemy can be our Nineveh that's requiring an obedient action that we're not ready to act upon. Giving God first place in our lives by obeying His call puts us on our way to our Nineveh.

Escaping to the sleepy little fishing village of Tarshish can be a running away from God without ever leaving home. Many of us go to Tarshish religiously. We do all the right things for the wrong reasons. We sing and pray while living our lives without any thought of what God would have us do in His kingdom on earth. Like Jonah, we go our own way carrying bitterness in our heart toward others and lie to ourselves, saying that it's not an attitude that God is concerned about.

When we become Christians, God begins a character transformation to change us from prideful, judgmental, self-centered persons to get us to join Him in loving all people and sharing with them what He has done for us. We cannot help anyone until these attitudes are changed.

Father, deliver me from evil—the evil of prejudice and bitterness toward any person or group different than me. Just as Jonah ran from Your command to give Your message to those he hated, show me if I'm guilty of the same attitude that would cause me to run from an opportunity to tell someone about You.

MEMORY CHALLENGE

How can a wicked man know that he will live and not die?

DAY THREE

Disobedience Hurts Others

Read Jonah 1:4-5.

Jonah was a prophet proclaiming God's message to Israel. Because of his refusal to obey God's command to go to Nineveh and warn them of God's judgment, he was out of fellowship with God. He failed to remember that obedience to God's will is not an option but rather an obligation and an opportunity.

1. How did the Lord begin to get Jonah's attention?

2. How did the sailors react to the violent windstorm?

The sailors called out to their gods in the hope that they could exert some influence on whichever god had become disturbed enough to send the storm. They were calling out for assistance, not repentance. The more gods they contacted the better, because different gods were appeased in different ways.

The ship Jonah sailed on was probably a large merchant ship. A ship making the 2,000-mile trip to Tarshish may not return for three years. The ship would have had a crew of 12 or a bit fewer. Cargo typically consisted of grain, wine, and olive oil.

3. From Psalm 107:23-25, 29, describe what the merchants on the ships saw as they sailed the sea.

Jonah's disobedience to God endangered the lives of the sailors aboard the ship.

4. How has someone's disobedience to God hurt you or your loved ones?

5. How has your disobedience hurt someone? If the Holy Spirit prompts you, share with your group your experience so that it may help others.

We must never forget, as Jonah did, that we have a great responsibility to obey God's Word, because our sin of disobedience will hurt others around us. When Jonah disobeyed, the Ninevites were hurt because they were left without God's message of hope that the Lord wanted delivered via Jonah. The crew members on the merchant ship were in danger of losing their lives because of the great windstorm sent by God in His attempt to get Jonah's attention to again direct him to Nineveh.

The sin of disobedience disrupts lives. Sin does not bring peace; it brings turbulence. Throughout the world we see where sin has disrupted friendships, marriages, ministries, churches, schools, businesses, cities, and nations. Betrayal in friendships, unfaithfulness in marriages, hypocrisy in Christian ministries, pride in churches, violence in schools, dishonesty in businesses, graft in cities and ego-centered political power struggles in governments are all sins against society as a whole.

Humanity casually accepts the seriousness of its disobedience to God's commands, wanting to forget that none of us lives to himself alone (Romans 14:7). The guilt of one person affects many lives. We have seen the misconduct of a nation's leader weaken the moral conduct of a nation. A drinking or speeding driver can leave devastating results on many families. The violence of a Timothy McVeigh can destroy families and burden society with millions of dollars of expense. An adulterous parent scatters a family and brings lifelong problems to children. The disobedience of one person compares with one seed of a dandelion, which brings forth hundreds of other seeds when it takes root and in time multiplies without boundaries.

6. Thought challenge: As you thoughtfully read each of the acts of the sinful nature listed in Galatians 5:19-21, consider how others are affected by a person who is guilty of these acts.

7. Prayerfully continue reading Galatians 5:22-23, describing how you respond when the fruit of the Holy Spirit is seen in a godly Christian.

MEMORY CHALLENGE

List God's three requirements for a wicked man to live and not die.

DAY FOUR

Jonah, Disobedient Prophet

Read Jonah 1:6-17.

In today's lesson we find Jonah asleep while sailors on the ship are frantically fighting to keep the ship afloat during a fierce windstorm. Jonah's sleeping while others are desperately working and praying upsets the captain of the ship.

1. What instructions did the captain give to Jonah, the disobedient prophet and sleeping passenger?

As a prophet of the one true God, Jonah should have been the first to assume the responsibility of prayer, but instead, he was the last. One living in disobedience to the Lord does not like to pray and would never be anxious to join others in prayer. Jonah needed to be awakened to the danger they were in.

Do you have loved ones and acquaintances who need to be spiritually awakened to the danger they're in today? It's often a difficult and thankless task to love someone enough to confront him or her about his or her lost soul.

> An immortal soul is beyond all price. There is no trouble too great, no humiliation too deep, no suffering too severe, no love too strong, no labor too hard, no expense too large, but that it is worth it, if it is spent in the effort to win a soul.
>
> God loves the soul more than all creation. He fashioned it after His own image, and made it like unto Himself. Every soul has departed from God and gone astray, and God has bought every soul back again with a price.
>
> That price was in, and through, and by Jesus Christ. God loves every soul with an everlasting love.[1]

Am I my brother's keeper? (Genesis 4:9). Do I have moral obligations toward others?

2. Record phrases from the following passages that indicate our responsibility to others.

   Isaiah 58:10

Ezekiel 22:30

Ezekiel 34:6

3. Ask God to reveal to you any step you can take to encourage an unbeliever to turn from his or her sinful life and accept Jesus as Savior.

After casting lots, the sailors determined that Jonah was responsible for this great storm.

4. How did Jonah identify himself to the sailors?

5. As the sea was getting rougher and rougher, what was Jonah's answer when the sailors asked him what they should do to calm the sea?

Jonah's answer clearly showed that he was no coward. He confessed his guilt as readily as he had professed his faith. He chose to drown rather than let others perish for his disobedience. He probably saw his death in the sea as the Lord's judgment. Yet in his religious belief, Jonah limited his glorious God into the narrow confines of a God for only the Jews.

The pagan sailors came to a final decision that since God had sent the storm to punish Jonah, He had not planned on harming others on the ship. They reasoned that Jonah alone should bear the consequence of his disobedience and acted on his advice by throwing him into the sea.

6. What were the results of the sailors' throwing Jonah overboard?

The immediate calmness of the sea convinced the sailors that the Lord of Israel was the true God. Forsaking their individual idols, they made a sacrifice of thanksgiving and vowed themselves to Israel's God.

Even in punishment Jonah was not forsaken by God. To be swallowed by a great fish would not be the method we would choose to be rescued, but it was God's divine act of kindness to bring Jonah safely ashore to accomplish God's command for him.

MEMORY CHALLENGE

If a wicked man turns away from all the sins he has committed and ________ _______ ______ decrees and does what is just and right, ________ __________ __________ __________; he will not die.

Ezekiel 18:21

DAY FIVE

Jonah, Man of Faith

Read Jonah 2:1-7.

Chapter 2 is Jonah's prayer from inside the great fish. He was surprised at finding himself alive after this frightening experience and gave thanks to God for his escape from death.

1. From verse 2:

   What phrase reveals that Jonah pictures his place in the belly of the fish as though he had been buried alive?

   What phrases indicate this is a prayer of thanksgiving, not a prayer for deliverance from the fish?

Jonah knew God's concern for people—that was the reason he rejected God's command and ran away. Now that he was in a desperate fight for his life, it was this same understanding of divine love that led him back to God. Even from inside the fish, Jonah's prayer reached God.

2. Who in the Bible encourages you to have faith when you need to believe in a difficult circumstance?

When we think of Jonah, we do not associate Jonah's life with great faith. We usually think first of the fish and Jonah's miraculous deliverance from the fish. Because of Jonah's bad behavior in refusing to go to Nineveh, we forget the rest of his story. Jonah has given us a great example of faith. He had everything against him. He had sinned against God, and his circumstances as he ran away at sea became impossible. But Jonah repented and clung tenaciously to God and received God's blessing of deliverance. Not many illustrations of faith in God's Word will exceed Jonah's example to encourage us to never let go of God regardless of how difficult our situation may be.

Jonah's prayers were filled with Scripture, especially the Psalms. When our prayers are not answered, can it be we need to be praying in a more effective way? Filling our prayers with Scripture gives them the power and authority of God's Word and His promises. To pray with Scripture is to pray according to the Word of God. Failure to learn and know the Word will leave our prayers unanswered.

4. Record Proverbs 28:9.

Jonah's prayers reflect the fact that he knew the Scriptures well.

5. Record phrases from Psalms that Jonah used in his prayer:

   Jonah 2:2—*In my distress I called to the Lord, and he answered me.*
   Psalm 120:1—

   Jonah 2:3—*All your waves and breakers swept over me.*
   Psalm 42:7—

   Jonah 2:4—*I have been banished from your sight.*
   Psalm 31:22—

   Jonah 2:7—*My prayer rose to you, to your holy temple.*
   Psalm 18:6—

   Jonah 2:9—*I, with a song of thanksgiving, will sacrifice to you. What I have vowed I will make good.*
   Psalm 50:14—

Anytime you read the 48 verses in the Book of Jonah, don't fail to see his great example of faith in his prayer of chapter 2. It can encourage you in any situation.

Jonah's prayers were answered because he prayed

from his knowledge of and faith in God's Word. Determine to let your prayers include more and more of the Word of God.

MEMORY CHALLENGE

If a wicked man turns _______ _______ _______

_______ *he has committed and keeps all my decrees and*

does _______ _____ _______ _____ _______, *he will*

surely live; he will not die.

Ezekiel 18:21

DAY SIX

Jonah, Repentant Prophet

Read Jonah 2:8-9.

1. In your opinion, what was an idol in Jonah's life that caused him to forfeit the grace and mercy of God?

Jonah knew why he was in trouble and was being punished. He admits there were idols in his life that robbed him of the blessing of God (2:8). One of Jonah's idols was his intense patriotism. He was so concerned for the protection and prosperity of Israel that he refused to be God's messenger to their enemies, the Assyrians. He wanted God to be God of Israel only.

An Israelite and God's prophet, Jonah had been commanded by God to preach to Gentiles, the Ninevites. This is another instance showing that it is God's will that His people lead the Gentiles to repentance.

2. In the following passages summarize how other Israelites had ministered to Gentiles:

   1 Kings 17:8-9, 19-24 (Elijah)

   2 Kings 5:1, 10, 14 (Elisha)

   Mark 7:26-30 (Jesus)

John 4:7-10, 25-26 (Jesus)

Acts 10:1-28 (Peter)

Acts 28:16, 28-31 (Paul)

3. Jonah declares that with a song of thanksgiving he will sacrifice to God (2:9). Summarize the following passages about thanksgiving and praise to God:

   Psalm 50:14-15

   Hebrews 13:15-16

> In refusing to go to Nineveh, Jonah had failed miserably to serve God because Jonah was not willing to sacrifice for God. Jonah would sacrifice for himself—he gave up time, effort and money to pursue a journey to Tarshish. But he would not do that to do God's bidding. He would not sacrifice his will, his interests or his reputation to go to Nineveh. So he failed to serve God. But now his prayer reveals a much different heart attitude. He is willing to sacrifice unto God.[1]

He would now be willing to give his time, effort, and money in serving God. He would no longer live the self-centered life that was another one of Jonah's idols.

In our lives today we fight similar temptations. Our time and our money are not easy to sacrifice. Do you have difficulty with materialism? Is sacrificing money a problem for you? True acts of sacrifice are our expressions of gratitude to God. They are not efforts to appease a God of wrath. With Jonah's declaration of sacrifice, he made a complete commitment to God's will for his life.

> Unwillingness to sacrifice is one of the biggest hindrances to serving God. . . . People may give, they may even tithe, but they still do not sacrifice in their giving. . . . The tithe is not the rule. Sacrifice is. Jesus forcefully drove home this truth when He was in the Temple with His disciples watching as offerings were being cast into the treasury (Mark 12:41-44). The rich "cast in much," but then a poor widow woman came along and only cast in "two mites." Jesus said the poor widow "cast more" into the treasury than the rich. Why? Because she sacrificed, and they did not. They gave out of their "abundance" and she gave out of her "want." . . . A man who makes $1,000 a week must give $100 to tithe. But he still has $900 left for himself. A man who makes $100 a week must give only $10 to tithe. But he only has $90 left to live on. The tithe of $10 will be a sacrifice for this man, but giving $100 is no sacrifice for the man making a $1000 a week. So what equity is that in making the poor to sacrifice, but not the rich? You may tithe and think you are doing very well when in truth you are a miser and cheap.[2]

At the conclusion of Jonah's prayer, it is evident that the chastisement for Jonah has made him a changed man. He is ready to be God's obedient servant once more. Chastisement hurts, and it can be very severe, as in Jonah's life. Its ultimate purpose will justify much pain, for no cost is too great if it results in restoring one into a good relationship with Almighty God.

MEMORY CHALLENGE

Prayerfully thank God for His restoration as you quote Ezekiel 18:21.

Jonah

■ A study of Jonah 2:10—4

LESSON 2

DAY ONE

God of a Second Chance

Read Jonah 2:10—3:2.

We are not told where the great fish deposited Jonah. No location is given for the "dry land." It is assumed that it was on the coast of Israel. We do know, however, that wherever Jonah was, the Lord was there. Although God was not pleased with Jonah, He never once deserted him throughout his rebellion. It was God who controlled the storm, custom-made the great fish, and rescued Jonah from the depths of the Mediterranean Sea.

1. Record the first phrase of Isaiah 43:2.

2. Record the last phrase of the following verses:

   Joshua 1:5

   Hebrews 13:5

There are times when Christians, like Jonah, are not obedient. Satan wants us to believe that there's no hope for recovering and that our ministry can never be restored, but Jonah shows us that our God is the God of a second chance.

3. Record Micah 7:8.

4. From the following passages, summarize God's forgiveness of His followers and the restoration of His plans for them:

   Genesis 12:10-20; 13:14-17

MEMORY CHALLENGE

Ezekiel 18:22

None of the offenses he has committed will be remembered against him. Because of the righteous things he has done, he will live.

Genesis 27:1, 19-24 and 28:10-15

Exodus 2:11-12 and 3:7-10

Matthew 26:69-74 and John 21:15-19

5. Record God's command to Jonah in Jonah 3:2.

God's original command to Jonah is repeated. The same God, the same command, with the same purpose.

With Jonah's opportunity for a second chance, we see a demonstration of God's grace. When Jonah disobeyed God's command, he did not merit another opportunity. Nobody does. But thankfully, in God's great mercy, Jonah is given another chance to respond honorably to God's command. Where would any of us be today if it were not for the unmerited grace of God that has allowed us second and third and fourth chances? How many times did you hear the Good News of salvation before you responded and received Jesus Christ as Savior? How merciful God is to all of us! How many times have you failed Him and gone back to Him in repentance, knowing He would accept you if you turned from your sin and asked forgiveness?

6. Record 1 John 1:9.

7. Summarize the following verses:

Psalm 32:5

Psalm 51:1-2

Jonah had experienced great suffering when he disobeyed God. Is there a lesson for us to learn in his experience? In obedience to difficult assignments, can we believe there will be fulfillment and blessing with the discipline and requirements of the task? The place of an assignment, the pain, the unknowns in the fulfilling of our commitment may be overwhelming at times, but the joy of obedience and the pleasure of working with the Lord make it rewarding and worthwhile.

Now you've got my feet on the life path, all radiant from the shining of your face. Ever since you took my hand, I'm on the right way (Psalm 16:11, TM).

The basis of Jonah's disobedience was the forgiving character of God. Jonah knew that if the Ninevites repented, God would forgive them. In the depths of the sea, Jonah had trusted in that forgiving character of God to rescue him and forgive him for his rebellion. He asked for a second chance.

DAY TWO

The People Repent

Read Jonah 3:3-5.

God could have sent another prophet to preach to Nineveh, but God knew there were lessons that Jonah could learn there.

1. What did Jonah do on his first day in Nineveh?

When the Word of the Lord came to Jonah the second time (3:1), God told him that He would give him the message he was to proclaim to Nineveh (3:2).

2. Record Jonah's proclamation to Nineveh.

How could a Jew, who believed and worshiped the only true God, convince these idolatrous Gentile Ninevites to believe his proclamation? Jonah had to face the possibility that he could be a victim of the horrible atrocities of the Assyrians. Facing these concerns, he nevertheless boldly preached in Nineveh in obedience to the Lord.

3. From 2 Corinthians 3:4-5 record phrases explaining Jonah's confidence to proclaim God's message.

In times of obeying God's challenges, we hear the encouraging truth that the will of God will never lead us where the grace of God won't keep us and the power of God won't use us. He is our confidence and our sufficiency. Praise His Name!

We have not been given any additional details to Jonah's message in Nineveh. The crucial thing is that Jonah obeyed God and went to Nineveh, declaring the message as God gave it to him. God did the rest.

It is noteworthy that God was giving Nineveh 40 days before they would be overthrown. Throughout Scripture the number 40 is identified with testing or judgment.

4. How was the number 40 used with the following?

   Noah (Genesis 7:4, 12, 17)

   Jewish spies (Numbers 13:25; 14:34)

   Nation of Israel (Deuteronomy 2:7)

   Goliath (1 Samuel 17:4-16)

The 40-day delay of divine judgment upon Nineveh gave all the people time to hear Jonah's warning and repent. In order to reach the greatest number of people, Jonah probably stopped at various places as he weaved back and forth through the markets and small streets. He would have included areas at the 12 gates and several places near the temple area. There would have been specified times during the day when significant announcements could be made.

Jonah's message was one of coming judgment, which was common for a prophet. The prophet in the ancient world should not be seen as a missionary. The prophet had the responsibility of delivering whatever message God gave him for a designated audience. A missionary's call is to convey God's message of salvation and give opportunity for repentance. In Jonah's message there is no call for repentance or command to turn from their false gods and evil deeds. He was in Nineveh to deliver God's message—and was alarmed and shocked at the results. He had not anticipated the immediate response of the people.

5. How did the Gentile Ninevites respond to God's warning and humble themselves in repentance?

When the people accepted Jonah's words as a message from God, they became greatly concerned. As conviction of their sins was acknowledged, they proclaimed a fast and put on sackcloth as a symbol of their humility and turning to God. Sackcloth was a dark cloth made from the long dark hair of the oriental goat or camel. It was coarse and ugly, not fit for normal wear. It was often worn to show sorrow, humility, and shame over one's sins.

Do you feel as though a past mistake would keep you from being used in the Lord's service? Like Jonah, you may again be asked to carry out His work. If you have doubts or fears, cast them aside in the name of Jesus. Be open, receptive, and available to hear Him. He who has ears (to hear His voice), let him hear.

MEMORY CHALLENGE

Why would God not remember our offenses?

DAY THREE

The King Repents

Read Jonah 3:6-9.

1. Record the actions of the king when he heard of Jonah's proclamation and the repentance of the citizens of Nineveh (3:6).

Conviction is defined as making one conscious of his or her guilt. As Jonah proclaimed God's warning, conviction of their sins caused the people to repent. The king's concern for the people and his concern of judgment of the city of Nineveh caused him, in desperation, to issue an extreme decree.

2. How were animals included in the decree?

Anyone around farm animals knows how cattle let their hunger and thirst be known. There is continuous bellowing and bawling. In Nineveh there would be a constant reminder of the possible overthrow of their city and the need for their repentance of sin in hope that God would change His mind.

By fasting and putting sackcloth on their animals, as well as themselves, the king and the Ninevites symbolized the unity of humanity and nature in their humbling before God. They had been convicted of their cruelty to other people, especially prisoners of war, and they knew that at the end of the 40 days, disaster would be brought upon them unless God relented by accepting their repentance for the wrongs they had done.

3. What was the hope of the Ninevites (3:9)?

The Gentile king of Nineveh believed the Lord's greatest desire was not to destroy people but to save them. Like Jonah and the sailors when they were in the violent storm at sea, the king of Nineveh and the people did not want to perish. Their fasting, praying, and humbling of themselves before God was a cry to Him for mercy. They hoped that God's great love and compassion would cause Him to change His plan and spare the city, but they had no assurance that they would be saved.

4. There are other instances in the Old Testament of God's conviction. Tell what circumstances caused His conviction in the lives of the following:

   Adam (Genesis 2:17; 3:8-10)

   Joseph's brothers (Genesis 37:27; 42:21-22)

   Israel (Exodus 32:31—33:6)

   David (Psalm 51:2-4)

5. Why would a holy God give the cruel Ninevites an opportunity to repent? Record phrases from the following passages for the answer:

   1 Timothy 2:4

   2 Peter 3:9

Jonah was angry at God because the Assyrians received undeserved forgiveness. In the Book of Job, Job was angry at God because of undeserved suffering. When have you been angry at God because of something that you felt was undeserved? Does that describe how you feel today?

With the hope of helping others who are hurting in their anger, a lady named Ginger has given us permission to include her story of an earlier time in her life when she ran from God.

I've been a Christian for 10 years and 8 months, but I've known Jesus my whole life. I've even loved Him from afar. But I had not had a life-changing encounter with Christ.

You often wonder why preachers' kids go off the deep end. Sometimes I think it's because they see a different side of the church. So I decided I didn't want any part of the church or God. And I wanted to see what the world had to offer me. So I left home thinking that I could finally do what I had wanted. I was free. No one was going to be looking over my shoulder. Peace at last. But God was always watching. And there was never peace, only darkness. A darkness so deep and so vast. I often felt that I was drowning in my own sin. It was at that lowest point in my life, when I was listening to a Michael W. Smith tape that my brother had given me, when God started to whisper my name.

I know my parents have prayed for me since the time I was conceived, but it wasn't until they had to totally release me to God that they could see the true power of prayer. For now, prayer was the only thing they had left. That was when I finally came to the point where I had to come home. And they welcomed me with open arms. But when I did, I felt that I was like the Pharisees when Jesus called them "white-washed tombs." They looked good on the outside, but they were full of dead men's bones. I was broken inside, but pride kept me from Jesus. I felt like I needed to pick up the pieces. What I didn't understand is—God wanted me broken.

So I asked my mom if I could have devotions with her, and she read from the 25th Psalm. Verse 7 says, "Remember not the sins of my youth and my rebellious ways; according to your love remember me, for you are good, O LORD." Verses 16-18 say, "Turn to me and be gracious to me, for I am lonely and afflicted. The troubles of my heart have multiplied; free me from my anguish. Look upon my affliction and my distress and take away all my sins." Then we also read about the sinful woman who washed the feet of Jesus with her tears. And Jesus said about her, "Her sins, which are many, are forgiven; for she loved much" [Luke 7:47, KJV]. And at that moment I felt how big God's grace really was. It was bigger than my sins. It was a love so big that it melted away the pride, the anger, the hurt. I was finally able to see Jesus, and I could never be the same again.

As I wrote out my testimony, God kept bringing to mind the words to "Amazing Grace." The second verse says, "'Twas grace that taught my heart to fear, / And grace my fears relieved. / How precious did that grace appear / The hour I first believed!"

As you read Psalm 25:7 with Ginger, are your reminded of unforgiven sin in your past or a rebellious spirit that causes you to feel lonely and afflicted? With His amazing grace He calls you to come to Him in confession and repentance. His amazing grace, love, and forgiveness long to give you another chance.

MEMORY CHALLENGE

None of the offenses he has committed will be remembered against him. Because ____ ____ __________ __________ ____ ____ ____, *he will live.*

Ezekiel 18:22

DAY FOUR

God Relented

Read Jonah 3:9-10.

1. Explain in your own words the decree of the king and his nobles in Jonah 3:7-9.

2. Summarize similar instances:

   Exodus 32:1-14

   Jeremiah 18:1-8

   Amos 7:1-6

3. *When God saw* ______ ______ ______ *and how they* __________ ________ ________ ______ ______, *he had* ______________ *and did not* ________ ________ ________ ______ ______________ *he had* ____________ (3:10).

The third chapter of Jonah is a fast-moving account of Jonah's walk through Nineveh. As we read it, we understand that there was a mighty stirring of God's Spirit in the great Gentile city. We know the king of Nineveh heard Jonah's message and led the citywide movement of repentance as he and the whole city put on sackcloth and ashes. They called on God; everyone turned from his or her evil ways and violence. The king and his nobles expressed hope in the last sentence of their decree: *Who can tell, God may turn and revoke His sentence against us [when we have met His terms], and turn away from His fierce anger so that we perish not* (3:9, AMP).

Repentance done in hope with faith is heard by God. The people repented, and God relented! The Lord changed His mind in response to the people's confession. That gives us the assurance that God is against sin but is 100 percent for us. The moment we turn to Him, He is waiting with forgiveness and grace. It is a time of new beginning.

God changes His mind as the individual changes his or her conduct. When a person repents of his or her wrongs and does what is right in God's sight, the basis of God's divine judgment no longer exists.

The Book of Jonah was written for Israel and all of God's people everywhere who will repent and believe. From reading about this reluctant prophet, we must determine to obey God, doing whatever He asks and going wherever He leads. It should cause us to answer the penetrating question "How do I respond to God's Word and His will for me?"

Like Jonah, when we refuse to obey His Word and His will for our lives, we will be disciplined. The great blessing of God's love and mercy is shown when we see God's grace given to Nineveh and Jonah. Though Nineveh was a wicked city, God gave its citizens an opportunity to be spared from His declared judgment of them. Though Jonah was a rebellious and disobedient servant, God did not let him go. He forgave him, used him to save Nineveh, and then patiently tried to help him overcome his anger by explaining His forgiveness of Nineveh. The Book of Jonah assures us that God is the God of a second chance even for rebellious nations and prophets.

MEMORY CHALLENGE

How does God regard our past sins when we turn from them, obey His laws, and live a righteous life?

DAY FIVE

Jonah Complains

Read Jonah 4:1-3.

1. How is Jonah described in 4:1?

2. Record the phrase in which Jonah is saying in effect, "I told you so!"

3. From Jonah 4:2, list the attributes of God that Jonah expresses.

4. Joel delivers a similar message to Judah. From Joel 2:12-13, record the phrases that warn us that God wants our attitude toward Him, not just our outward actions, to be correct.

5. God will not accept a change of lifestyle without true inward repentance. Summarize 1 Samuel 16:7.

Only God can see our inner person, and only He can accurately judge people. Everyone can see your face, but only God and you know what is happening in your heart. Are you at peace with the steps you're taking to grow in your walk with Him? Is there an area in your life you know that God would be pleased for you to change?

> If God wanted only to save the city of Nineveh, the book would have ended at Chapter 3. But there was still more work to do, for God wanted to save His servant from himself. . . . The basic problem was that Jonah was not completely yielded to God. His mind knew God's truth, and his will obeyed God's orders; but he did not do the will of God "from the heart." He obeyed only because he was afraid of what God might do to him. His was not a ministry of love.[1]

6. Complete this thought from Ephesians 6:6—

Obey . . . not only to win . . . favor . . . but like slaves of Christ ____
____.

Jonah had obeyed the Lord by going to Nineveh and proclaiming God's warning, but his heart's attitude had not been changed to care about them or to love them. He was filled with hate toward them and was eagerly looking forward to their destruction. The prophesied 40 days were over, and the great city had not been overthrown.

Have you been grudgingly surprised when someone you viewed as corrupt turned to God? Realistically, we must see ourselves as a narrow-minded Jonah if we cannot rejoice over every person whom God forgives. Jonah was happy when God saved him but angry when Nineveh was saved.

7. Read the parable in Luke 15:11-32. Explain what the older brother had in common with Jonah.

Although Jonah had been miraculously saved from death by the unmerited mercy of God, he was not about to rejoice when the hated enemies of Israel experienced the same transforming mercy. He knew that if Nineveh survived, they could be the ones God would use in His judgment against the rebellious nation. Jonah's national loyalty to Israel overpowered his spiritual loyalty to God.

God knew that Jonah did not want Nineveh to receive His mercy. He was opposed to Jonah's attitude and would try to correct it.

8. In his anger what request did Jonah make (4:3)?

Another prophet made the same request. Who was this prophet (1 Kings 19:1-4), and who was he afraid of?

Seeing thousands of Israel's fierce enemies seeking God angered Jonah. His prediction of Nineveh's destruction was not going to happen, and Israel's cruel enemy had been spared. He felt rejected by God.

9. Record Hosea 11:5.

Israel had not been delivered from her great enemy. She must continue to pay heavy tribute and would be unable to become a stronger and more respected nation, as Jonah had thought would be possible without Assyria. Because of their acceptance of his message, Jonah now felt he had been responsible for the future destruction of Israel. He felt personally discredited and humiliated by God's response to the repentance of Assyria. Jonah wanted to die. His reputation as prophet among the Israelites was more important to him than the salvation of thousands of repentant people. He had let hatred of the Gentile Assyrians become such a driving force in his life that their escape from the threatened destruction robbed his life of all meaning.

Ask God to bring into your thoughts the person you dislike the most. Begin to pray for this person, and thank God for loving him or her. He will change your heart and attitude.

MEMORY CHALLENGE

Jonah's life would have been pleasing to God if he had repented of the hatred in his heart and lived a life of righteousness.

Personalize Ezekiel 18:22:

None of the offenses ____________ *[your name] has committed will be remembered against* _______. *Because of the righteous things* ____________ *[your name] has done,* ________ *will live.*

DAY SIX

God Explains

Read Jonah 4:4-11.

1. Visualize Jonah as you read 4:5-6. If you enjoy sketching, draw a picture of him as described in these verses.

2. Write a condensed version of verses 4:7-8.

3. Name the concern in Chapter 4 of the following:

   Jonah:

   God:

4. What is the primary concern of your life today? Is it more like Jonah's or God's?

5. Record Matthew 6:33.

In the closing passage of the Book of Jonah, God teaches Jonah through a living parable, using a vine, a worm, and a scorching east wind. He began to reason with Jonah. Using the parable, God explained an important truth: if Jonah could be so upset about the withered vine that had grown with no participation from Jonah, didn't God have the right to show loving concern for people whom He had created?

The Book of Jonah ends with God speaking to Jonah. God did not tell him it was wrong to be disappointed that the vine had withered, but He explained that Jonah's concern should have included people who were of greater value in God's sight than a vine and cattle, who were spared the suffering that would have included them if Nineveh had fallen. Jonah had no pity or sympathy for the people or the animals. God mentioned them to Jonah to show how his religious exclusiveness had made him blind to the needs of others, how he thought only of himself—and as the parable progressed, it revealed his increasing unrighteousness.

> What the Lord says to Jonah, He says to all. . . . If they are angry, not with men but with sins of men, if they hate and persecute, not men but the vices of men, they are rightly angry, their zeal is good. But if they are angry, not with sins but with men, if they hate, not vices but men, they are angered amiss, their zeal is bad.[1]

God created all people equally; all humans are unique and special creations formed by the Lord himself. In heaven there are no ethnic groups, no races, no distinctions as we have made on earth (Galatians 3:28). The Bible speaks out clearly against prejudice and racism. From the Old Testament we read warnings against mixing with foreign nations, but the emphasis was on purity of worship, not on racial differences. The New Testament clearly teaches that all races are God's creation and that Jesus Christ died for all, regardless of culture or skin color (Ephesians 2:11-18).

Jonah felt justified in hating the enemies of Israel. Throughout the centuries we have seen hatred of one country against another. Jesus died to destroy all the barriers of hostility that sin has created and continues to create between people (Colossians 3:5-11). The followers of Christ should be color blind and politically tolerant. We can take a stand for our own beliefs without hating those with whom we strongly disagree. Regardless of background, race, gender, political party, or church preference, the presence of Christ in the lives of believers makes us all one in Him.

The Book of Jonah ends with Jonah's complaining to God that he wants to die. The last scene shows a pouting Jonah, angry at God and all that's happening as he looks on Nineveh hoping for its destruction. Scripture does not tell us what happened to Jonah, but other passages of Scripture and secular history tells us what happened to Nineveh.

760 B.C.—The estimated year that Jonah gave God's warning to Nineveh.

723-722 B.C.—Brutal Ninevite soldiers attacked Israel. Going through the nation, they deported people, scattering them throughout their other conquered nations. Strangers were brought into Israel to resettle the land.

612 B.C.—About 150 years after God's warning through Jonah, the destruction that God had threatened came upon Nineveh. The Babylonians became the new world power.

As we end our study of Jonah, what will we remember? From chapter 1 we learn that it's essential in Christian service to be content with the will of God. When we're angry with God, everything in life becomes troubled. We say and do selfish things. Running away becomes more important than ministry, especially if it's in a place that's far from home, to people in a different culture. Chapter 2 gives an example of praying anywhere, anytime, and knowing God hears and answers. In chapter 3 God gives Jonah a second chance and blesses the ministry of an imperfect servant. There's power in God's Word; it can convict and convert sinners. In chapter 4 a vine, which has no soul, becomes more important than people with lost souls. Comfort becomes more important than ministry. But God is long-suffering and tenderly works with us to bring us to himself.

Scan the Book of Jonah or your completed lessons and recall ways that Jonah's story has touched your life. Talk to God about how you want to use these truths in your life as you walk with Him each day.

As never before we should see the value of saying, *I desire to do your will, O my God; your law is within my heart* (Psalm 40:8). We must walk with God, not run from Him.

MEMORY CHALLENGE

Write out Ezekiel 18:21-22.

Introduction to Esther

Esther is the heroine of an ancient historical book of the Bible set in the splendor of the Persian Empire at its height of power in the 5th century B.C. This is a dramatic and rather gory tale of love, hate, and palace intrigue. The story probably derives from the many reports of persecution and deliverance in the Persian era, handed down from generation to generation.

There was no more powerful man on earth at that time (485-465 B.C.) than the Persian King Xerxes. He stripped every conquered nation of its riches, using them chiefly to enhance his own magnificence. He demanded exorbitant taxes and gifts of the subject peoples that he might live in the splendor for which Persian rulers were famous.

Xerxes had ample cause for pride in his winter capital. Of the three cities that served as his headquarters during the year, Susa was perhaps the finest. Persepolis, some 300 miles southeast of Susa, was the official capital, the site of the most imposing temples and the burial place of the kings. Occupied only in the spring months, it was in Persepolis that political and military leaders from the entire empire—127 provinces—gathered to pay taxes to the king's treasuries. Ecbatana, 200 miles north in the highlands of Media, was the royal refuge from the fierce summer heat of Susa.

As a nation, Persia became the modern nations of Iran and Iraq. As an empire, Persia was a vast collection of states and kingdoms reaching from the shores of Asia Minor in the west to India in the east. It reached northward to southern Russia and in the south included Egypt and the regions bordering the Persian Gulf and the Gulf of Oman.

It was a harsh land of deserts, mountains, plateaus, and valleys. The climate was arid with extremes of cold and heat. Gold, silver, wheat, and barley were native to the area.

The Persian Empire is important to the history and development of civilization. It had major effects on religion, law, politics, and economics. The impact came through the Jews, the Bible, contacts with the Greeks, and through Alexander the Great's incorporation of ideas and architecture of the Persians.

Politically, the Persian Empire was the best organized the world had ever seen. By the time of Darius I (522—486 B.C.), the empire was divided into 20 political units of varying size and population. They were governed by Persians who were directly responsible to the king. Good administration required good communications, which called for good roads. The geographical center of what was then the largest empire ever assembled, Susa was a natural crossroads for travelers on the great highway system from Asia Minor to northern India. It was a bustling cosmopolitan center. Long-haired, perfumed visitors and envoys from Babylonia, itinerant Greek scientists, Jewish merchants, and Persian infantrymen in coats of mail and long trousers jostled one another on market-lined streets.

The Persians treated most of the conquered kingdoms, including Judah and Israel, with a leniency exceptional in that period. Subject peoples were allowed to worship their own gods and live by their own customs. Countries that had not actively fought the Persians kept their own forms of government and maintained armies, though under Persian officers.

This is the setting for the drama of Esther.

Bible Study Series

Esther

■ **A study of Esther 1**

DAY ONE

Celebrating at the Palace

Read Esther 1:1-8.

1. After reviewing the Introduction to Esther, how do you picture Persia?

2. List materials that had been used to construct the luxurious setting for the banquet (Esther 1:6).

3. Summarize verses 7-8.

4. What warning is given in Amos 6:4-7 for living this lifestyle? (Use *The Living Bible* for this answer.)

5. What blessing for a nation is stated in Ecclesiastes 10:17?

6. What danger for a nation is given in Proverbs 31:4-5?

The Book of Esther begins with an account of an opulent party staged by King Xerxes in his winter palace at Susa, located in modern Iran, not far from the Iraqi border. Guests were all the important persons that he governed, invited so that he could display the riches of royal glory and the splendor and pomp of their king.

Xerxes no doubt reveled in the magnificence of his banquet hall at Susa. Kneeling bulls sculptured in pairs topped the tall, slender, distinctive Persian columns that

MEMORY CHALLENGE

Galatians 6:7

Do not be deceived: God cannot be mocked.
A man reaps what he sows.

supported the roof. The walls of many-colored glazed bricks were decorated with reliefs showing fantastic-winged bulls and other mythological creatures, and Persian archers and spearmen.

Materials from every corner of the empire—ebony and silver from Egypt, gold from Asia Minor, ivory from Ethiopia, and semiprecious stones from east of the Caspian Sea—had been used to construct the luxurious palace. Darius had brought in foreign laborers and specialized craftsmen to complete the edifice, and they embellished it with designs from their native lands.

King Xerxes sat in his royal place of honor at the center of the table in his great banqueting hall, and all about him were gathered the 127 princes of his far-flung empire.

> This convocation of princes of Xerxes probably took place at the very time when he was planning his ill-fated invasion of Greece. For 180 days, the king has been engaged in showing those assembled the riches of his glorious kingdom and the honor of his excellent majesty. And now in the last seven days a great banquet has been in progress. Xerxes is surrounded by his 127 princes, all gorgeously dressed in their appropriate robes, with their gems and jewels and tiaras sparking in the light that glows from the myriad candles and the massive candelabra that hang from the ceiling. . . .
>
> In accordance with the known heathen custom of those times, we can imagine slaves and eunuchs passing food and liquors to the guests. In the minstrels' galleries sensuous music floats down with the sounds of the harp, psaltery, timbrel, flute, cornet and dulcimer. Fountains throw spray from their basins and the sweet incense . . . fills the air.
>
> On a central platform dancing girls in flimsy garments whirl beguilingly about in an Oriental dance. Seven days have passed, and they are still eating, drinking and dancing. Those overcome by drink and fatigue are carried out by their slaves on litters.[1]

Perhaps Xerxes was saying to himself, *What more can I do to entertain and excite these guests?* His solution to this question changed the future for the Jewish people.

The Book of Esther is the drama of a nation. It tells of a nation's deliverance. Not once does the name of God appear in these 10 chapters nor does the word "providence"; yet God and His providential intervention permeate every chapter and event in this book.

Who could know that what started out as a lavish feast designed to impress the high military on the eve of a strategic battle would in fact be scene one: the stage setting for a historic chain of immortalized events?

DAY TWO

Vashti

Read Esther 1:9-12.

1. Where were the women during the banquet of the king?

2. On the seventh day of the banquet, what startling request was made of Queen Vashti?

3. The king's request places Vashti in a difficult position. What factors would she be considering in her decision?

   What was her answer?

4. What happened when a request was made at an earlier time *while they were in high spirits?* Briefly summarize Judges 16:25-30.

5. What was the king's reaction to Queen Vashti's response to his request?

6. What can be observed about the king's character?

7. What is your opinion of Queen Vashti?

8. How have others in the Bible refused to be intimidated by ungodly requests?

   Nehemiah 6:5-12

   Jeremiah 26:7-15

   Daniel 6:7-10

It was when the heart of Xerxes was inflamed with wine that he made his shameful and infamous request concerning Vashti the queen. That is the long and sad history of strong drink, ever since it left Noah—God-fearing, unashamedly obedient Noah—uncovered and disgraced in the presence of his sons and beside the very altar he had built to God (Genesis 9:21).

However commonplace and fashionable it may be to drink liquor, let it never be forgotten that the effect of liquor is to stir up the lower passions of one's nature and to relax one's caution in acting on them. In a moment of such relaxation, when the stimulation of strong drink has weakened the natural resistance to evil, young men and young women have responded with an act of sorrow or shame that can never be reversed.

Startled by such a wicked and unprecedented command, the drunken lords sat up in eagerness to await the coming of the renowned queen. To do proper honor to the royal Vashti, the king sent seven VIPs from his court to escort her to the feast. But far from proudly leading their queen into the presence of her husband the king, the seven returned to report, amazingly for those times, that Vashti refused to attend his banquet. She would not expose herself to the lascivious gaze of Xerxes and his drink-inflamed guests.

Had the king been sober, he would not have considered such a breach of custom, for he knew that Eastern women lived in seclusion and that such a request that he made in his drunken condition amounted to a degrading insult. What Xerxes demanded was a surrender of womanly honor, and Vashti was unwilling to comply. What the king sought would have infringed upon her noble, feminine modesty, and there she had the right to disobey. A wife need not and should not obey her husband in what opposes God's laws and the laws of feminine honor and decency.

Vashti had world-famed beauty. There is nothing wrong with being beautiful, but Vashti lives forever in history not because she had beauty but because she had character, respect for herself, without which her beauty would have encased an empty shell of a woman. She knew the cost—dismissal from the court, exile, perhaps death itself—but she loved honor, her soul, more than life. Vashti's refusal lost her the crown, but it made her immortal. It made Esther immortal too. For as we will see, had it not been for the courageous "no" of Vashti, Esther would not have become queen and probably would have continued her life in obscurity. Esther has societies and guilds and women named after her, but do you know of any named for Vashti? She may be equally as deserving as Esther.

MEMORY CHALLENGE

If a person is being deceived, what warning must we give him or her?

DAY THREE

Seek God's Counsel

Read Esther 1:12-14.

1. Are the king's *wise men* mentioned in verses 13 and 14 the same as his trusted servants (eunuchs) named in verse 10?

   How do you see their different roles in the life of the king?

2. What was to be the fate of the wise men of King Nebuchadnezzar in Daniel 2:12?

3. Name the wise man referred to in Jeremiah 10:6-7.

4. How is God described in Isaiah 28:29?

5. In his drunkenness, instead of honestly facing his arrogance and pride that caused him to make an inappropriate request, the king became excessively angry. His quick temper identified him as a fool. Record the phrases from the following passages that affirm this:

   Proverbs 12:16

   Proverbs 14:17

   Proverbs 14:29

6. What guidance from the following scriptures is given on coping with anger?

   Proverbs 15:1

   Ephesians 4:26

   Ephesians 4:31

   James 1:19-20

In these first passages in the Book of Esther, Xerxes shows himself to be a foolish king. With a feast lasting six months with unlimited royal wine, he corrupts his leaders, promotes laziness, drinks excessively, acts unwisely when drunk, and allows his anger to get out of control.

The king's dignity was publicly offended by Vashti's refusal to obey, and some strong measures to enforce his authority were certain to be taken. Wise men were regularly in attendance with an oriental monarch to give advice. They knew all the Persian laws and customs.

7. Why is advice from others needed? Refer to Proverbs 12:15.

8. How valuable is wise counsel? Refer to Proverbs 25:11.

9. Record God's promise to His children from Psalm 32:8.

"I don't know what to do."

"Can you tell me what you would do?"

These are common cries that we hear often. Counselors are in great demand—one on one, in newspapers and magazines, on the radio, on television, and via the Internet. But there's a difference between wise counsel and misleading advice. Well-meaning instruction can lead to destruction. Of all wisdom, God's is the best, for His is given with a perspective of eternity. We would do well to seek advice more often from the source of divine wisdom: God's Word. God wants to be your Source, not your last resort.

We are wise to recognize our own inadequacies and to admit our limitations rather than to foolishly think we have none. It's important to seek advice from those who love God and have a knowledge of the Bible and are faithful, godly, honest, and trustworthy. When evaluating their advice, it is your responsibility to yourself to check it against the truth of God's Word. If it contradicts the Bible, avoid it at all costs.

10. How do I give good advice to others? Refer to Philippians 4:8-9.

In giving advice to others, have pure motives, point to God's Word, and don't use it as an opportunity to lecture. Pray about what you want to say, and have the other's best interest in mind. Words are like medicine; they should be measured with care, for an overdose may do more harm than good.

As we study further with King Xerxes, we will see that he was advised to use manipulation and intimidation for the women in his kingdom in reacting to Queen Vashti's refusal to obey his command.

MEMORY CHALLENGE

Do not be ________: *God cannot be* ________. *A man* ________ *what he* ________.

Galatians 6:7

DAY FOUR

Falsely Accused

Read Esther 1:15-16.

1. What was the accusation against Queen Vashti (verse 15)?

2. How was the accusation enlarged?

3. Record Proverbs 14:25.

4. Read Genesis 39:5-23.

   What was the false accusation against Joseph?

   What was Joseph's punishment?

   What was the prison warden's treatment of Joseph?

5. Read the following.

Psalm 105:16-22; record verse 19

Psalm 108:11-13; summarize verse 13

Psalm 109:1-5; summarize the prayer

When the king summoned his wise men and angrily asked them what he should do with the disobedient queen, they insinuated that the fault was all the queen's. They further stated that by her refusal, she had wronged not only the king but also every official and citizen throughout his empire. This, of course, was a lie. The one responsible for this disturbance was the king—and the king only.

Does it ever fail? When a person traps himself or herself by reacting in a situation in which his or her pride has been offended, he or she usually strikes out at a loved one. Why do we do this? Ray Stedman in *A Pair of Queens* explains, "It's simply the nature of sin. This is the story of human life—and this is what happened here. When this king was lifted up in pride, he began to fancy that the glory was his—that it was all his making and his doing, and then in his pride he sent for the one who ought to have been reserved for the intimate communion of his own private life to make mockery of her before all. But he found it could not be done."[1]

Joseph's story (Genesis 39) parallels Queen Vashti's when he was falsely accused. Potiphar's wife resented Joseph for not yielding to her evil desire and accused him of seducing her. Potiphar, the Egyptian officer, was enraged at Joseph when she told him her lies. Joseph was a foreigner in a strange land and a slave with no status. There were no witnesses. Joseph was put into prison, where he had no voice.

Vashti was falsely accused and blamed for refusing the king's request. Joseph was falsely accused and blamed for refusing the wife of Potiphar.

Scripture does not inform us of Vashti's life after the king banished her from his presence. Commentators have suggested that it is quite probable that she continued to live in the royal household—possibly in the harem—stripped of her place of royalty but clothed in her own personal dignity and integrity.

We're left with no doubt concerning Joseph's future. God's plans for Joseph were being fulfilled on His schedule and in His timing. The most important test a person may have to pass before he or she is greatly used of God is to be punished when falsely accused at a time when in truth he or she is radically obeying God.

That is exactly what happened to Joseph. He was put into prison because he was falsely accused while doing everything right.

6. Summarize 1 Peter 2:20.

Joseph continued to do everything right in prison. He was faithful wherever God put Him.

If as a child of God you have been hurt by being falsely accused, God feels more deeply about it than you do. Like Joseph and Vashti, you're probably in a place in which you're unable to defend yourself. You're in this place because God wants to step in and show you that what is absolutely impossible with people is possible with Him.

If you will only be quiet, say nothing, and do not try to manipulate the situation, God will be moved, and He will act. God loves to do that.

For most of us it takes a lifetime to fully believe Romans 8:28—*We know that in all things God works for the good of those who love Him, who have been called according to His purpose.*

This verse in the *Amplified Bible* reads, *We are assured and know that [God being a partner in their labor], all things work together and are [fitting into a plan] for good to and for those who love God and are called according to [His] design and purpose.*

In a difficult time we should never despair, never be despondent. We are to be simply a channel of helpfulness to others. Joseph is our example—he remained faithful in the daily tasks. Like Joseph to his fellow prisoners, we're to have more sympathy and feel more tenderness toward others. Begin to believe and rejoice that you will be an overcomer.

MEMORY CHALLENGE

When I sow peace, I will reap _________.

DAY FIVE

Women—B.C. and A.D.

Read Esther 1:17-20.

1. Summarize Memucan's analysis of Queen Vashti's refusal to obey the king and the resulting repercussions throughout all of the Persian and Median empire (1:17-18).

2. In his exaggeration of the reactions to the queen's decision, how did he advise the king to take action to eliminate future controversy?

Like Memucan, we can imagine the worst-case scenario, scramble to solve problems that will never exist, and exhaust ourselves in the attempt—simply because we are afraid. We are not to fear. We are to remember how Jesus faced the devil in the wilderness and conquered (Matthew 4:1-11) with "the sword of the Spirit, which is the word of God" (Ephesians 6:17). Look on every fear not as a weakness but as a very real temptation to be attacked and overthrown.

3. Knowing that fear is a temptation to not love and trust God in your situation, how are you encouraged by the promise in 1 Corinthians 10:13?

Always look for an open door and the blessing on the other side as you overcome the temptation to fear. To have the decree written in the laws of Persia and Media made it permanent—it could never be changed. Commentators have written that Memucan's suggestion for the king to write the decree in the laws of Persia and Media indicates his fear that the king would wish to change the law in the future when he longed for Vashti to be reinstated as his queen. If this would happen, Memucan and the six other advisers would then face a queen who would not be pleased with their advice to Xerxes that she must be banished and replaced by someone who is better than she.

Would Vashti's single act of insubordination actually have ruined family life throughout the empire? Or was this an excessive response to Vashti's imagined influence? Ironically, Vashti received as punishment exactly what she had possibly wanted in the first place: freedom from coming before the king.

For us it may be difficult to understand the significance of Vashti's refusal. But things were far different in those days, as they remain today in many Eastern cultures. In this instance, not only was the king put down by one in his own household, but it was by a woman. Even if she was the queen, a woman had no right to make a choice. A woman was an inferior being, a part of his property, a slave.

G. Campbell Morgan relates that "the story reveals the place which women occupied outside the covenant of the chosen people. She was at once the plaything and the slave of man."[1]

Yet our culture, too, regularly places women in the position of Vashti, a position in which they feel demeaned by a society that tends to value their appearance more than their character. Many contemporary women who read the Book of Esther relate more readily to Vashti than to Esther. They can relate to the woman who stood up to her husband who valued her only as an object of beauty rather than as a person worthy of respect and love.

Could there be a greater contrast between the attitude of Xerxes and that of Jesus? Even women who might have lost their right for respect found Jesus to be someone who saw them as people, not as objects.

4. Summarize Luke 7:36-39.

Jesus did not see before Him a sinner or a prostitute; He saw a woman who loved, who was forgiven, and who had been saved by her faith.

5. Summarize Luke 7:44-50.

Jesus did not see an object of lust or scorn, but a person who could give and receive love. Of all the benefits and blessings of Christianity, none is more profound than the changes in the status and role of women. In a very real sense, Jesus Christ is woman's best friend.

Unfortunately, Christians are not immune to the offense of devaluing women and men. Sometime we act more like Xerxes than Jesus—when we see others only as objects of admiration or lust. But Jesus calls us to see people as valuable individuals, not as toys for our enjoyment. His example reminds us that people exist to be loved, to love others, and to give delight to God.

In his Pentecost sermon Peter shows the outpouring of the Spirit upon Christians, fulfilling the prophecy of Joel 2:28-29. *In the last days, God says, I will pour out my Spirit on all people. Your sons and daughters will prophesy, your young men will see visions, your old men will dream dreams. Even on my servants, both men and women, I will pour out my Spirit in those days, and they will prophesy* (Acts 2:17-18).

The Holy Spirit empowers both men and women for the ministry of Christ. Through Christ we experience an empowering freedom to be shared with others. We see people as Jesus sees them, and by His Spirit we receive power to empower others—both women and men.

MEMORY CHALLENGE

Do you have an experience from your life that proves this verse to be true?

DAY SIX

Decisions

Read Esther 1:21-22.

1. Xerxes drank wine to the point of drunkenness. In that intoxicated condition, he ordered Queen Vashti to do something inappropriate. When she disobeyed, he banished her from her royal position because of his prideful, wounded, selfish ego and in agreement with the fears of his advisers that the women in his empire would now be influenced by Vashti's act of disobedience.

   Summarize:

   Proverbs 20:1

   Proverbs 23:31-33

The king was suffering the consequences of unwise decisions. One decision was made while he was intoxicated; the other was an overreaction to a woman's disobedience, and that decision could never be changed.

There are consequences to any decision we make. A decision—right or wrong—can set in motion a series of events that may continue far into the future. We can see this in the king's life. Like him, we, too, often think only of the immediate consequences. We need wisdom for making decisions.

2. What are some principles of wise decision-making? Summarize the following passages:

   Make sure you have all the facts.
   Proverbs 1:5

   Be open to new ideas.
   Proverbs 18:15

Seek God's guidance.
1 John 5:14

Seek advice from trusted friends.
Proverbs 12:15

Make sure your decision is not based on values that contradict God's Word.
Psalm 119:98

How do you know you've made a good decision? Does the result of your decision produce good fruit?
Galatians 5:22-23

You will consistently make good decisions if you're spending high-quality time in God's Word and acting upon His principles.
Hebrews 5:14

Knowing the Scriptures and gleaning His wisdom gives us guidance in our decision-making and provides us with the discernment we need to make correct choices.
Psalm 25:4

Even if we don't always make the best decision, God has the power to make the decision work for good.
Romans 8:28

3. Summarize God's promises to us:

Psalm 23:3

Proverbs 3:6

Father, like King Xerxes, we have all made unwise and wrong decisions. Today some of us are living in the pain and despair that have resulted from those wrong choices. Your Word in Jeremiah 29:11 assures us You have a plan for each of us to give us hope and a future. We know also that Satan has a plan for us and that he goes to and fro across the earth searching for anyone he can destroy. He plans to keep us in hopelessness with no future. By faith in the One who gave His life for us so that we could have life and have it abundantly, we trust You to lead us in paths of righteousness. You have promised that You order the steps of us who obey You. Thank You for the answer, in Jesus' name.

MEMORY CHALLENGE

Quote Galatians 6:7 from memory.

WISDOM OF THE WORD Bible Study Series

Esther

■ A study of Esther 2—3

DAY ONE

Life in Susa

Read Esther 2:1-7.

Chapter 2 begins after the campaign to Greece in which the Persians were soundly defeated. After his defeat, King Xerxes returned in deep dejection to his palace in Susa. The king began to miss his queen. He was a lonely man. He was also remembering that in his anger he had removed her from his presence with a decree that could not be rescinded. He had great numbers of women in the harem for his sexual pleasure, but he wanted a wife, someone to be near him and comfort him, someone who would be his companion, someone to care for him long term.

1. King Xerxes had been inordinately proud of Queen Vashti. His thinking of her now with regret cast gloom over the entire court. As the king's attendants served him, they observed his loneliness. They felt something had to be done to counteract his dejection. What was their suggestion?

2. What does God say about being alone (Genesis 2:18)?

3. The Bible shows us that each of us needs the comfort and help of others. Summarize the following passages.

   Illustrated in the life of Moses
   Numbers 10:29-32

   Emphasized by Solomon
   Ecclesiastes 4:9-12

   Practiced by Jesus Christ
   Matthew 26:36-38

   Shown by sending forth the disciples
   Luke 10:1

   Recognized by Paul in his missionary work
   Acts 13:2

   In cooperation with God
   1 Corinthians 3:6-10

MEMORY CHALLENGE

Galatians 6:8

The one who sows to please his sinful nature, from that nature will reap destruction; the one who sows to please the Spirit, from the Spirit will reap eternal life.

Xerxes saw few of his multitudes of subjects face to face. In the interest of security, a curtain isolated the throne room from the rest of the hall, which was 250 feet square, with beams of the famous Lebanon cedar. Only a select few—the seven nobles who were his closest advisers—could approach the king without invitation. He needed a companion to share his grief of losing his queen and being defeated in his campaign to conquer Greece. In his pagan empire he did not worship the God who could be his Comforter.

This is the account of the unending restless search of humanity for something to satisfy the deep need of the heart. It begins with the king seeking to satisfy his troubled soul with an elaborate search for someone to fill the vacuum of his life. This reflects the entire story of human life without God: the seeking, restless, dissatisfied soul—never daring to be alone with his or her own thoughts, always demanding something to anesthetize the pain of his or her own loneliness, always looking for some form of continual pleasure, anything to avoid sensing his or her loneliness.

King Xerxes could have agreed with Proverbs 19:22—"What a man desires is unfailing love."

> Each of us craves utterly unfailing love: a love that is unconditional, unwavering, radical, demonstrative, broader then the horizon, deeper than the sea. . . . Interestingly, the Word of God uses the phrase "unfailing love" 32 other times, and not one of them refers to any source other than God himself. . . . It is not His will for anyone to perish, and since the only way to have eternal life is to receive Him, God created us with a cavernous need that we would seek to fill until we found Him."[1]

The king did not know to search for God.

4. In this passage we are introduced to the two major characters of the Book of Esther living in Susa. Who are they, and what is their relationship?

There is no greater institution, no better group of people to affect positive changes in the world than the family. There is no better place to learn the essential principles of life; and nowhere can the truths of God's Word be more effectively taught and modeled. Family is the environment that shapes a child for a lifetime. The Bible lists several genealogies, all recorded by family units, showing the family as central and fundamental to the development of people and nations. Family is God's creation.

5. From the following Scriptures record phrases relating to families.

   Joshua 24:15

   Psalm 127:3

   Proverbs 6:20-23

   Proverbs 22:6

   Proverbs 29:15

   Proverbs 31:27

Mordecai's devotion to the Jews of Babylonia indicates that he was faithful to Jewish customs while Esther lived in his home. Jewish children learn from their parents what God is like and pass it on to their own children. The same is true of a Christian's understanding of the character of God, with the family being the starting place for instructing our children. Some of our most powerful lessons will be taught to our children as they watch us go through the struggles of life. Victory over perplexing problems teaches our children that God answers prayer and wants to provide power to face the challenges of life.

We need to develop in our children a hunger to taste, feed upon, and digest God's Word regularly in obedience to God's command in Deuteronomy 6:6—*These commandments that I give you today are to be upon your hearts.* The result is good spiritual growth for our next generation and those to come.

6. What instructions are given to parents in Deuteronomy 6:6-7?

When Cyrus conquered Babylonia some 50 years earlier, he had given all the Jews permission to return to their Palestinian homeland. But they had been well treated by the Babylonians. Many of them had prospered as merchants and craftsmen. New generations had grown up without personal memory of their fathers' country. The majority, therefore, had no desire to journey to the arid hills of Judah. With the new freedom of travel afforded under Persian rule, however, many Jews moved to other parts of the empire, including Susa. Mordecai was one of the many Jews living in Susa.

Day-to-day family life in Susa was not much different from the life of their fellow Jews in the homeland. One day each spring their homes were filled with the odors of roast lamb and bitter herbs for the ritual Passover meal, commemorating the ancient exodus from Egypt. Young children still heard the tales of Israel's past heroes, triumphs, and tribulations. Little suspecting that other such threats could arise in Susa, they were reminded how often their forebears had suffered persecution.

Mordecai had a young cousin named Esther. When her father and mother died, Mordecai adopted her as his own daughter. Esther regarded Mordecai as her own father. This fact not only explains the parent-child relationship between Mordecai and Esther but also heightens the emotional power of her story—a beautiful young woman who rises from the low social status of an orphaned immigrant to the highest possible position as queen of the empire.

DAY TWO

The Secret

Read Esther 2:8-14.

We have learned two things about Esther: she was an orphan girl adopted by Mordecai, and she was now a young woman of incredible beauty. At this time she knows nothing about palace politics or a lonely king or what the future holds for her. She is living the typical life of a Jewish family exiled in Babylonia and is residing in its capital, Susa.

1. Why had Esther moved from the home of Mordecai?

2. What special privileges did Esther receive at the palace?

3. What special instructions did Mordecai give Esther?

4. How did Mordecai show concern for Esther?

5. What was the routine for the young ladies in the harem until they returned to the second harem?

Esther the Jewish orphan became Esther the queen of Persia. Every province of Xerxes' empire was searched for its most beautiful women, those who were possible candidates for the crown of the queen of Persia. Along with other beautiful young virgins from the empire, Esther was gathered into the palace at Susa under the care of Hegai the eunuch. In the months that followed, young women of every color, from dusky beauties of Ethiopia and India to proud princesses of conquered kingdoms—some aspiring to be queen, others fearful—spent a night with the sated sovereign and were in the morning assigned to the house of the women where they remained as the king's concubines (2:14).

It was a common practice in the ancient world for kings to have harems of concubines. These women did not have the status of wives but were actually servants. They were to provide the king with sexual pleasure and, in some instances, with children. Since the king entertained a new virgin every night for several years, it was unlikely that he would remember one whom he had known days, months, or even years before. In reality, the women in Xerxes' contest were sentenced to a life of unfulfilled loneliness.

Esther did not reveal to the Persian authorities her Jewish background. It is likely that this factor could have eliminated her from royal competition. Although we are not told why Mordecai advised Esther to keep her lineage a secret, the intent in verse 10 is to portray her not as scheming or deceitful but rather as obedient to her adoptive father. Esther was not only beautiful but was also a faithful and submissive daughter. Additionally, her ability to be discreet about her lineage discloses her wisdom. Esther's secrecy about her ethnic background is an important detail in the development of the rest of the story. If Xerxes had known she was a Jew, either he would not have selected her as queen or he would not have brought the Jews to the point of extinction.

Mordecai continued to be concerned about the fate of Esther (verse 11). He was a typical worried father who loved his adopted daughter and longed for her well-being.

Most of us have loved ones for whom we long for their well-being. Are you a father, mother, sister, brother, or friend who faithfully prays for those for whom you're concerned? Do you feel like the boy's father in Mark 9:24 who first proclaimed, *I do believe,* and then in the same breath cried out, *Help me overcome my unbelief!*? Faith is a gift from God (Ephesians 2:8). Faith is a growing process as we daily renew our trust in God. Nothing is too difficult for God. Believe it!

MEMORY CHALLENGE

If we sow to our sinful nature, what do we reap?

DAY THREE

Queen Esther

Read Esther 2:15-23.

1. Three times Esther has found favor with someone (verses 9, 15, 17). What does this tell us about Esther?

2. Summarize:

   Proverbs 11:16

   1 Timothy 2:9-10

   1 Peter 3:4

3. How do you visualize that Esther's life, role, and rights as queen would be different from the women remaining in the harem?

Of all the maidens gathered in the palace of Xerxes, Esther was perhaps the only one who worshipped the true God, though this fact is not recorded. Educated as a daughter in the house of Mordecai, a wise and devout Israelite, she had probably learned from him the truths about God treasured by her people. She may have been the only one who had not worshipped idols or some heathen god. From her infancy, devout Jewess that she was, she probably bowed to Jehovah, and in this wealthy Persian kingdom she was in touch with a power not counted in terms of marble, silver or gold.[1]

There is a question of the king having the right to marry Esther. She belonged to a special race, the Jews, a race forbidden by their own law to marry with another race. Yet in this foreign land, by the sovereign overruling grace of God, Esther is brought before the king. He recognized in this lovely girl the answer to the empty restlessness of his life, and he set the sign of royalty upon her head, granting her authority in the kingdom. Throughout the kingdom was seen an immediate effect—the lifting of the burdens of taxation and the distribution of royal gifts with liberality. So great was Xerxes' joy that he sponsored another giant feast, this time in Esther's honor. When he was angry, he raged uncontrollably; when he was glad, he celebrated lavishly.

4. Record Proverbs 19:12.

5. Where could Mordecai be found?

6. How did the king learn that his life had been threatened?

Once Esther was crowned queen, she managed to remain loyal to Mordecai while also being loyal to the king (verses 21-23). So we see in chapter 2 that Esther illustrates several wise maxims—as an obedient child who listens to her father, as a prudent speaker who knows when to keep silent, and as one who remains loyal even in conflicting situations.

For Mordecai, to be sitting in the king's gate tells us that he is a judge, for legal transactions of the ancient world were settled at the gate of the city.

Mordecai's integrity caused him to choose to reveal the assassination plan against the king even though he knew he would risk retaliation. God wants us to be people of godly, consistent character, and that means choosing to do what is right in all situations.

God laid the groundwork for His plan to save His people when it would be ordered for them to be annihilated (chapter 3). Esther was now the queen of Persia. Mordecai, as judge at the gate of the city of Susa, was in the right place to overhear the scheme to assassinate the king. God would use Esther's royal position and Mordecai's place at the gate to fulfill His purposes.

MEMORY CHALLENGE

Who will reap eternal life?

DAY FOUR

Mordecai Stood Alone

Read Esther 3:1-5.

A member of King Xerxes' government within the palace has received a promotion.

1. Who is Haman?

2. The evil deeds of Haman create the central conflict in the Book of Esther. Haman exemplifies most of the traits that are given in Proverbs 6:16-19. List these seven traits:

Haman, an Agagite, is a descendent of King Agag of the Amalekites. Exodus 17 records that King Amalek, a descendant of Esau, fought against Israel as they passed through his land when Israel was on their way through the wilderness from Egypt to Canaan. From this time throughout Scripture, Amalekites were always enemies of all that God wanted to do.

3. As Satan hated God, so . . .

Cain hated ____________________ (Genesis 4:8)

Ishmael hated ____________________ (Genesis 21:9)

Esau hated ____________________ (Genesis 27:41)

Amalekites hated ____________________ (Exodus 17:8)

Haman hated ____________________ (Esther 3:6)

From the New Testament, Herod the Great, who in his attempt to kill Jesus ordered the death of all the children in Bethlehem two years of age and under, was also a descendant of Esau, making him kin to Haman.

King Xerxes disregarded Haman's non-Persian status and promoted him to a high position within the government, equivalent to a prime minister of today.

4. What authority is designated to Haman?

5. How will God treat those who curse His Chosen Ones (Genesis 12:3)?

We will see in Haman's life the proof of Genesis 12:3.

6. What was happening at the king's gate that troubled all the king's servants?

7. How did they choose to solve the problem?

8. How did Haman react after he observed Mordecai's insubordination?

9. Have you chosen to take a stand at a time when no one agreed you were doing the right thing?

Whenever Haman entered or left the king's palace, everyone gave him reverence and bowed down—all but one man, Mordecai, who refused to bow or give Haman honor in any way.

Mordecai was a man with character. He had principles and was true to them. He would not go against his principles to reverence any man—especially a wicked man like Haman. Without character, without loyalty to principle, of what value is a man?

We must admire Mordecai's standing erect while the crowd at the city gate lay flat on their faces. While there is no record of his faith in God, his actions prove him to have been a godly Jew who would not revere anyone but God.

We have had those in our nation that have had to make a choice when confronted by angry gunmen. It was a time to renounce God or be willing to die. In these circumstances, to take a stand and declare loyalty to God places a life in danger of martyrdom. Certainly we know these were the plans of Haman for Mordecai and all the Jews in the Persian Empire.

Nineteen-year-old Jeremiah Neitz stood when those around him were hiding or fleeing for their lives. A gunman was firing between 65 and 100 rounds of ammunition at those attending a youth rally at Wedgwood Baptist Church in Fort Worth, Texas, on September 15, 1999.

[Neitz] stood up and confronted the killer: "Sir, you don't have to be doing this." The gunman yelled at Neitz to shut up, punctuating his statement with profanity. "Sir, what you need is Jesus Christ." The killer pointed the gun at Neitz and cursed him. As Neitz relates the story, "I held my hands out to my side and said, 'Sir, you can shoot me if you want. But I know where I'm going. I am going to heaven. What about you?' The gunman would shout one last expletive, put the gun to the side of his head, and fire. . . . The gunman had ended his own life"[1]

God does not write a "happy ending" on earth for every courageous believer. Some of God's choicest saints have suffered and even died for Him. But God still writes the ending of our life story, even if it looks to us like failure. Radically obedient believers look forward with joy to the future God has planned for them. He has prepared a place for them to live eternally.

MEMORY CHALLENGE

The one who sows to please his __________ __________, from that nature will reap _________________; the one who _______ to please the ___________, from the Spirit will reap ____________ ____________.

Galatians 6:8

DAYS FIVE & SIX

Persecution —Past and Present

Read Esther 3:6-15.

1. Why do you believe Christians are harassed and persecuted for their beliefs?

2. Why do we sometimes waver about our beliefs when we feel intimidated?

3. When you know Christians and Jews are being persecuted and challenged in their beliefs, how are you strengthening and preparing yourself for such a confrontation?

Persecution of Christians had been a part of history from earliest times. As you read the following history of persecution, underline any thoughts you may want to discuss in your study group.

The First Martyr

We tend to focus on the New Testament when we think of martyrdom and why Christians are persecuted. This is understandable considering the persecution that befell the early church as they went out to evangelize.

However, we believe that martyrdom and why Christians are persecuted go back much farther, as far as the Book of Genesis, when Cain killed his brother Abel.

Genesis 4:1-15 relates the well-known account of how Cain's sacrifice to God was not accepted, as was Abel's. And for this, Cain took out his anger on Abel and killed him.

In Matthew 23:35, Jesus speaking to the Scribes and Pharisees, said, "That on you may come all the righteous blood shed on the earth, from the blood of righteous Abel . . ." [NKJV].

And in Hebrews 11:4, we read, "Through which he [Abel] obtained witness that he was righteous . . ." [NKJV].

Through these references we believe it is safe to conclude that Abel was the first martyr [witness] and that he was martyred for his "faith" and "act of righteousness." And from this, we believe all persecution derives.

Persecution will exist as long as God's children continue to engage in acts of righteousness in a sinful world (2 Timothy 3:12).

The Old Testament

The writer of Hebrews spoke of those "of whom the world was not worthy":

"Women received their dead raised to life again. And others were tortured, not accepting deliverance, that they might obtain a better resurrection. Still others had trial of mockings and scourgings, yes, and of chains and imprisonment. They were stoned, they were sawn in two, were tempted, were slain with the sword. They wandered about in sheepskins and goatskins, being destitute, afflicted, tormented—of whom the world was not worthy" (Hebrews 11:35-38 [NKJV]).

We often think of the prophets of old escaping persecution, like Daniel as he faced the lions. But even Daniel had to be willing to be ripped from limb to limb as he was lowered down in the den of lions refusing to deny his God. Not an easy task!

The New Testament

With the arrival of Christ came a new wave of persecution upon His birth announcement (Matthew 2:16).

Even before the crucifixion of Jesus, John the Baptist was beheaded (Mark 6:21-29).

After Jesus' crucifixion, Stephen was stoned while a man named Saul stood watching: "And they cast him out of the city and stoned him. And the witnesses laid down their clothes at the feet of a young man named Saul" (Acts 7:58 [NKJV]).

Before dying, Stephen looked up to heaven and saw Jesus standing. "But he, being full of the Holy Spirit, gazed into heaven and saw the glory of God, and Jesus standing at the right hand of God" (Acts 7:55 [NKJV]).

Regarding the fare of the apostles, with only the death of James recorded in the New Testament, we learn from early writings that all except for John were killed.

The Church (A.D. 54-304)

Nero was believed to have set Rome on fire and blamed the Christians. Some of the most hideous forms of persecution took place under Nero's rule. Christians were sewn into the skins of wild animals and thrown before fierce dogs. Others were covered with wax, setting these human candles on fire to help light Nero's garden.

Under Emperor Domitian, persecution continued. Domitian issued an order stating, "No Christian, once brought before the tribunal, should be exempt from punishment." During this time Timothy was beaten to death.

In A.D. 110, Ignatius, overseer of the church in Antioch, was fed to lions. Over the roar of the hungry animals, he was heard saying, "I am the wheat of Christ; I am going to be ground with the teeth of wild beasts that I may be found pure bread."

Following Ignatius' martyrdom, Adrian came to power, under whom about 10,000 Christians were put to death—many by crucifixion with crowns of thorns on their heads.

Under the rule of Emperor Marcus Aurelius Antoninus, Polycarp was martyred. He was tied to a stake in the marketplace. Wood was piled around him and set on fire but the flames did not touch him. He was then pierced with a sword. Other Christians were tortured during this time, experiencing horrendous tortures.

Persecutions continued under Emperor Lucius Septimus Severus and Emperor Marcus Clodius Pupienus Maximus.

In A.D. 249, a seventy-year-old Christian woman named Appolonia was tied to a stake to be burned. After the fire was set she begged to be set free. The mob, believing she would deny Christ, set her free only to witness her throwing herself back into the flames.

Persecution spread to Africa, Spain, France and Britain. Hatred of Christians continued to grow, as did the church. By A.D. 304, the persecution of Christians reached the peak of its magnitude and cruelty.

The Dark Ages

During this time the church lost much of its passion and began taking up pagan doctrines that would benefit church leaders. All who opposed were labeled heretics and swiftly executed.

About A.D. 1000, a man named Berengarius began preaching from the Scriptures gaining thousands of followers. Over the next 200 years many "reformers" were captured and burned at the stake. Others disappeared in dungeons.

In a continued attempt to stop those who opposed the "doctrines" of the organized church came the birth of the Inquisition. Each Inquisition was comprised of about twenty officials. But their methods were cruel and they had little cause for mercy among those accused of heresy.

There is no record of how many Christians fell victim to the Inquisition. It is believed millions. Despite the eventual decline in cruelty, the Inquisition remained in effect into the nineteenth century.

The English Bible

In 1380, a free-thinking theologian named John Wycliffe translated the first English Bible from the Latin Vulgate. He also called for the reform of the organized church.

Wycliffe died in his sleep in 1384, but 31 years later the Council of Constance removed his remains and had them burned. The ashes were thrown into the river in a vain attempt to eliminate his influence, but his legacy remained.

Around 1484, another man was born who changed the course of history—William Tyndale. Tyndale declared, "If God spare my life, it will not be many years before I will cause a plow boy to know more of the Scriptures than the Pope." And with that declaration, William Tyndale went into hiding and began translating the English New Testament from the original Greek.

Scripture in the English language was completely forbidden. Ten Christians were even burned at the stake for teaching their children the Lord's Prayer in English.

William Tyndale's new translation went into print in 1525 but was not completed until 1526. The English Bibles had to be smuggled in bales of cotton. Anyone caught possessing one was put to death.

In 1535, William Tyndale was arrested, and burned at the stake in October 1536. With the English Bible still illegal, his last words were "Lord, open the King's eyes!" His prayers were answered one year later when the King gave official permission to print and distribute the English Scripture (74 years before the first King James Bible).

China and the Iron Curtain

A few hundred years later, persecution became evident in Asia. The Boxer Rebellion started in 1899 when a secret society of Chinese, coined "Boxers" by the Western press, began a terror against Christian missionaries in China. Officially, the Boxers were denounced, but unofficially supported. Their activity continued through 1900.

Humiliated from the outside, the Chinese officials signed a peace treaty with the Boxers in September 1901, but not before 30,000 Christians and 250 missionaries were martyred.

Communism's father, Karl Marx, once stated, "The idea of God is the keynote of a perverted civilization. It must be destroyed."

Communism spread rapidly throughout the 1900's. With its spread came the destruction of churches and the imprisonment of Christians. During Communism's height, it was estimated that 330,000 Christians were killed each year. Millions of others suffered at the hands of cruel dictators like Enver Hoxha, Nicolae Ceausescu, and Mao Zedong.

During this time men like Pastor Richard Wurmbrand emerged from years of imprisonment, torture and solitary confinement to speak of the atrocities and overcoming faith of those who boldly faced death rather than deny Christ.

Today Christians continue to suffer under Communist ideology in countries like China, North Korea, Vietnam and Laos. Believers remain in prison and Christians continue to risk all to simply own a Bible.

Persecution Today

Even though persecution continues in a number of Communist countries, the greatest threat comes from Muslim nations imposing Islamic rule on its citizens. In many Islamic nations, one can be put to death simply for converting from the Muslim faith to Christianity.

In spite of the increased persecutions in Sudan and other Muslim nations, the church continues to grow at astonishing rates. The boldness of the believers mirrors that of the early church who rejoiced "that they were counted worthy to suffer shame for His name" (Acts 5:41).

The patterns of persecution and the testimony of faithful believers have surrounded the children of God for thousands of years. It is not an issue, or an event, but a faith-based reality for those who choose a life of faith and righteousness. As we enter the third millennium, may we be found worthy of its calling.[1]

To convince the king that mass murder of the Jews was necessary, Haman was forced to use every cunning approach his evil mind could connive. With a combination of exaggeration, flattery, lies, and bribery, he made his request to the king.

4. Have you been tempted to use half-truths and lies to convince someone of something you wanted him or her to believe?

Lies continue to be propagated by Satan today in the hearts of countless men and women and boys and girls who have allowed themselves to be persuaded of one of his biggest lies: that to give themselves back to the God who made them and to submit themselves to His sovereignty is to be robbed of the liberty that makes life really worth living.

5. 2 Corinthians 4:4:

The ________ *of this* _________ *has blinded the minds of unbelievers, so they cannot* _______ *the light of the gospel of the glory of Christ, who is the* ___________ *of* __________.

The king was sold out to Haman completely. It is probable that when entrusting this decree to Haman, the king was unaware that Esther was a Jew. His own ring would give authority to the death decree for his queen, Esther.

All the Jews were to be eliminated, including young and old, women and little children (3:13). Only total genocide would satisfy the wicked wrath of Haman.

The chapter ends abruptly with a strong contrast between the partying of the conspirators and the confusion of the people of Susa. The king and his Hitler have issued their decree, but God has not forgotten His people!

MEMORY CHALLENGE

Record Galatians 6:8.

Esther

■ A study of Esther 4—5

LESSON 3

DAY ONE

God's Chosen Ones Mourn

Read Esther 4:1-3.

1. Mordecai was mourning for the Jewish people. List three ways his actions demonstrated his sadness.

2. Why was Mordecai not allowed to pass through the king's gate?

Sackcloth is a garment of coarse material fashioned from goat or camel hair. The shape of the garment could have been either a loose-fitting sack placed over the shoulders, or a loincloth.

3. Choose a phrase from each of the following passages that expresses the reason for wearing sackcloth:

   Genesis 37:34

   1 Kings 20:31-32

   Isaiah 58:5

   Joel 1:4, 7-8

4. Who was wearing sackcloth in the following passages?

   2 Kings 6:26-30

   Isaiah 20:2

MEMORY CHALLENGE

Galatians 6:9

Let us not become weary in doing good, for at the proper time we will reap a harvest if we do not give up.

Isaiah 32:11

Jonah 3:6-8

Matthew 3:4

5. What does sackcloth symbolize in the following passages?

Isaiah 50:3

Revelation 6:12

Ashes, the powdery residue of burned material, often were associated with sacrifices, mourning, and fasting.

6. How were ashes used in the following passages?

Exodus 9:8-10

Numbers 19:9

7. What are ashes symbolic of in the following verses?

Genesis 18:27

2 Samuel 13:7-19

Daniel 9:3-5

Grief, humiliation, and repentance were expressed by placing ashes on the head or by sitting in ashes. Dirt, sackcloth, fasting, the tearing of clothing, and ashes visibly demonstrated a person's emotions. At times the ashes that remained from a sacrifice were kept and used for ritual purification. Ashes also symbolized the results of divine destruction and the devastating effect of God's wrath as shown on Sodom and Gomorrah (2 Peter 2:6).

8. How did Jews throughout all the provinces respond to the decree declared by the king?

The behavior of Mordecai and the Jews in every province where the king's command and decree arrived reflects their normal social custom of mourning and expresses the horror of the decree that had been issued against them.

A crisis does not make a person; it shows the character of a person. In spite of the danger involved in going against the king's command, Mordecai publicly displayed his grief and let people know his position. He would not stand by and do nothing when authorities were ready to slaughter innocent people and their children.

9. How do you as a citizen respond when laws are passed that you feel are wrong?

10. In the United States, the National Day of Prayer is scheduled on the first Thursday of May each year. Other countries may observe similar special days of prayer. As we recognize that the only hope for our individual countries is to appeal to the Lord for His mercy and grace, how will you plan to be part of such a day each year?

Record 2 Chronicles 7:14.

Mordecai could only go as far as the open square of the city, which was in front of the king's gate, because he was in a state of mourning and therefore ceremonially unclean.

Jews throughout the empire joined Mordecai. Such public expressions of grief may strike us as odd and inappropriate; however, Middle East cultures encourage much greater freedom in their expression of sadness. A visit to Jerusalem would not be complete without seeing the Wailing Wall. It is a wall about 160 feet long and 40 feet high. The lower part of the wall contains stones said to be from Solomon's Temple. Beginning in the 700s Jews assembled at the wall on the evenings before their Sabbath and before their feast days. In services at the Wailing Wall, the Jews recalled their traditions and sufferings, wailing and praying. They held nothing back, openly displaying their grief.

There was great mourning among the Jews, with fasting, weeping and wailing (4:3). There are several reasons for fasting. Like the Jews throughout the province of Persia, our primary time of fasting is when we're so burdened about something, so concerned about it, that we lose our appetite. Instead of physical hunger, there comes a deep, insatiable moaning, groaning, and longing for God. The end result is that we are more available to God. He can work through us.

God was aware of all that was taking place in Persia. No doubt many of the Jews were questioning why God would allow this to happen to them. Just because God permits evil to happen in the world does not mean that He is unconcerned or unwilling to help. When God is not allowed to rule, He overrules, and He always accomplishes His purposes.

Everything about Haman and his influence on King Xerxes was against God and His people. But God did not interfere, because He knew Haman's sins would ultimately destroy him and be used for the good of His chosen ones. As one of the first-recorded anti-Semites, Haman proved that they who curse the Jews are cursed of God.

DAY TWO

Esther's Challenge

Read Esther 4:4-8.

1. How did Queen Esther learn of Mordecai's mourning in front of the king's gate?

2. When Mordecai refused the garments from Esther in her attempt to replace his sackcloth, how did she proceed to obtain information from him to understand his actions?

3. What message did Mordecai want delivered to Esther?

4. Describe a personal situation in which God has placed you to do His will and to commit to acting in obedience with courage and integrity in that situation.

5. Give scripture passages that give you encouragement for continued obedience.

The Jews wore sackcloth and ashes when mourning, with hopes of averting national catastrophe. That was the Jews' way of immediately turning to their God for help. They sought God's protection and mercy before doing anything else.

6. What is your first response to tragic news?

When Mordecai learned the decree that the king had made through the evil influence of Haman, he was moved with deep sorrow. He cried out in heaviness of heart because he understood that the king did not realize all that was involved. Mordecai knew the people of God would be destroyed in every province of Persia. Also, he knew that the decree was an unchangeable law of the Medes and Persians, and the consequences of the king's decision were without possibility of being changed.

> Also, he wept out of sympathy for the king and his kingdom because of the sorrow they unwittingly brought upon themselves. Mordecai knew the Jews were under special protection from God wherever they were. As a Jew he knew the history of the race. He knew that no nation laid its hand upon the Jew in anger or in punishment with impunity. This is the thing that Hitler forgot.[1]

How was it possible that Esther did not know of the plan of Haman to annihilate her and her people? It is implied that she did not know of the king's decree that had already been delivered to the 127 provinces of his kingdom. This seemed impossible knowing Esther's position as queen. But verse 11 explains that she had not been called by the king for 30 days. Confined to her private quarters, Esther was not aware of what had happened the last month outside the palace. Only when her servants told her was she informed of Mordecai's mourning at the palace gate. Mordecai's refusal to accept clothing was evidence to Esther that his actions were caused not by a personal sorrow, but by an unusually urgent and desperate public calamity. He could have accepted the garments she sent and resumed his place of responsibility in the city gate.

With Esther's servant, Hathach, as courier, Mordecai answered clearly and specifically when Esther asked for an explanation of why it was that he was grieving. Mordecai gave her devastating facts regarding Haman's plot to destroy her people. He knew the exact amount of money that Haman had told the king he would put into his treasury; he also had a copy of the decree. He revealed the whole plan to Esther in specific, exact detail.

To counteract the decree that had been issued to annihilate the Jews, Mordecai directed Queen Esther to go to her husband *to beg for mercy and plead with him for her people* (verse 8). Although Esther was now the queen of Persia, Mordecai continued to relate to her as an authoritative father by commanding her to approach the king on behalf of all Jews.

At the instruction of Mordecai, Esther had remained silent about her Jewish heritage. With the grim extinction of the Jews in sight, Mordecai felt the only solution was for Esther to intervene *for her people* (verse 8). Her people! That meant she must reveal her Jewish origin. How would the king react? Would he feel she had deceived him? Did he hate her race as Haman and many others hated it?

Esther had been challenged by Mordecai, and she had to make a very difficult decision.

MEMORY CHALLENGE

What will we reap from doing good if we do not give up?

DAY THREE

Thy Will Be Done

Read Esther 4:9-14.

1. What was Esther's initial reaction to Mordecai's request that she go to the king on behalf of the Jews, and what factors would Esther have been considering in answering Mordecai's request?

2. List three facts used by Mordecai to persuade Esther that it was a worthy risk for her to make her request of the king.

King Xerxes was never without protection from unnecessary interruptions and annoyances and was guarded from the possibility of an assassination attempt. To appear in his presence unannounced, without the approval of his advisers, meant instant death unless the king held out his golden scepter to show his acceptance of them. Esther and Mordecai knew the risk for Esther to be willing to go to the king. Also, they knew that Queen Vashti had been banished from the throne because she had disobeyed palace protocol.

3. Esther's questioning of her responsibility to appeal to the king did not reflect weakness with her answer to Mordecai but showed she was considering Jewish wisdom in her decision. What advice is given in Proverbs 25:6?

Her reply to Mordecai was a reasonable reminder of the danger involved and the need for understanding of her relationship with the king. Even though it was especially dangerous for Esther to make an uninvited appearance before the king, Mordecai continued to be the authoritative father of the queen, commanding her to approach the king. She must have recognized that Mordecai was a man of unusual insight with special guidance—with his primary concern the fate of his people. Mordecai knew the God who had a plan for Israel that was being fulfilled as He had promised in the Scriptures.

Mordecai assured Esther that delivery and rescue would come. If not through Esther, it would come from another source. He was applying a principle that is true in every age: while evil may prevail because good people sit still, keep quiet, and do nothing, these good people suffer with the rest when trouble comes.

From another place (verse 14). Mordecai must have referred to God. Throughout the ages He had promised the Messiah would come through the Jewish people. Haman could not prevent this. Neither could Satan. Though the need for deliverance was urgent, Mordecai's trust in God was without question.

Would Queen Esther cooperate with God's plan, or would she fail? Was she prepared to lose her life for the deliverance of her people? Choices come into the life of every child of God—those to be made when God's purpose for their life is being revealed. They are both frightened and excited at the prospect as His presence waits to empower them. Fulfillment comes with the realization that they could never accomplish what they are being called to do. Death to all their own inadequacy is the beginning of living in the fullness of Christ as He enables them to accomplish all He calls them to be and do.

4. How does Matthew 16:24-25 instruct us?

Mordecai challenges Esther with the probability that Esther has a higher vocation than being queen of Persia. Could God have given her the royal position in order that she might be used in the rescue of her people? Are you being called by God's Holy Spirit to do a special work for Him?

> When Jeannie McCullough, the teacher of Wisdom of the Word Bible studies, came to the place in her life's journey where God was calling her to be radically obedient, it was a moment much like Esther's. Many fears filled her mind. Her husband was a pastor. What if obeying God might somehow conflict with what the church expected? What if the message God gave her to speak was too convicting and not well received by its members? They might never again have a church to pastor. Their family might even starve to death! And what about her disabilities? Surely God would not allow anyone to know about those!

Each of us at the moment God calls us to obedience will face an "Esther moment." Satan will fill us with fear. In fact, he will use the very thing we fear most in life—he'll will convince us that it will surely happen if we're obedient to God. Notice that the middle three letters in the word "obedience" spell "die." We must come to a point at which, in spite of our worst fear, we are willing to obey God and die to our will, no matter what the outcome. Our attitude must be like Esther's: *If I perish, I perish* (verse 16).

What is keeping you from being radically obedient? Does it cause you such great fear that you can't even discuss it with God, much less think about being obedient to Him? Has Satan convinced you with his intimidating conversations that if you are obedient to God, you will lose the very thing you love the most? You can rest assured that even if the worst that you could imagine did happen, God would be with you and see you through it (Romans 8:28). God cannot use you until you're willing to offer everything to Him. As Mordecai warned Esther, God would use someone else to accomplish His purpose if she were not willing.

Jeannie and her husband did not lose their church. For over 40 years they have always had a people to pastor. In fact, for the past 15 years her husband has been the senior pastor of one of the largest churches in their denomination. And God has given Jeannie a special teaching ministry in spite of her disabilities. Instead of trying to hide them, she has been an inspiration to others with learning disabilities, demononstrating that God can use them, teach them, and give them understanding of His Word.

Don't let Satan with his fear tactic keep you from experiencing God's best for your life. Let God have everything. And when you have nothing left, you'll be amazed at what He'll give back to you![1]

MEMORY CHALLENGE

Let us not become ________ *in* ________ ________,
for at the proper ________ *we will reap a* ________ *if*
we do not ________ _____.

Galatians 6:9

DAY FOUR

Fast Proclaimed

Read Esther 4:15-17.

1. Esther was now willing to risk her position, her life, and her future for her people. How did she begin to publicly identify herself with her people?

2. Record the three phrases of Esther's final decision.

3. How does Romans 12:1 reinforce Esther's decision?

In this decision we see the weak Persian woman, valued only for her beauty and submissive obedience to her foster father and her husband, the king, become decisive, courageous, and authoritative.

Chuck Swindoll explains that Esther's call to fasting implies that she would be waiting on her Lord in prayer during that time:

> That is what fasting is all about. . . . She was saying, "Pray for me. Fast for me. And my maidens and I will do the same. And we will see what God will do." In other words, she determined to wait on the Lord and allow Him to guide her thoughts and help her frame her words. . . . During a waiting period, God is not only working in our hearts, He's working in others' hearts. And all the while He is giving added strength.[1]

4. Read Isaiah 40:31 (from the NASB or TLB version), and list the benefits of waiting.

In Esther's time of waiting three days while fasting, she would gain new strength, get above the fear of danger, and begin to feel a stronger determination with extra energy and confidence.

5. Record phrases of encouragement from the following scriptures.

   Psalm 32:6-7

   Psalm 32:8

   Isaiah 41:10

   Isaiah 41:13

As she prepares for her encounter with the king, Esther must wait, fast, pray, think, and in quietness and confidence listen with her spiritual heart.

> Fasting is found 75 times in the Scriptures, 44 times in the Old Testament and 31 times in the New Testament. . . . The Bible does not tell us how to fast, how often to fast, or how long to fast.[2]

A partial list of those in the Bible who fasted:

Moses in the presence of God on Mount Sinai when he wrote upon the tablets the words of the Covenant, the Ten Commandments (Exodus 34:27-28).

The Israelites in time of defeat (Judges 20:26), in time of repentance (1 Samuel 7:6), in time of sorrow (1 Samuel 31:12-13).

David at the death of Jonathan and Saul and for the house of Israel, because they were fallen by the sword (2 Samuel 1:12).

Jesus in time of great temptation (Matthew 4:1-2).

Paul during his first missionary journey, to discern God's will and anointing (Acts 13:2-3).

Some of the lengths of fasts:

One day (Judges 20:26)
Twice a week (Luke 18:12)
Three days (Esther 4:16)
Seven days (1 Samuel 31:13)
14 days (Acts 27:33)
40 days (Matthew 4:2)

No instructions are given for the length of time for a fast. Christians should be willing to fast until they discern that God has completed His purpose for the fast.

It's good to exercise a discipline in which self is denied by saying no to the flesh and at the same time saying yes to the Lord. It means putting a priority on the Spirit instead of on the flesh.

MEMORY CHALLENGE

When will we receive a harvest for doing good?

DAY FIVE

God Saved the Queen

Read Esther 5:1-8.

1. The days of fasting and preparation were over. Esther began to fulfill her promise to Mordecai. Laying aside her garments of sackcloth, worn during the time of fasting, how did Esther choose to dress?

2. Pale but composed after her fasting, she came to the king *all glorious . . . within: her gown . . . interwoven with gold. In embroidered garments* (Psalm 45:13-14). Esther was dressed fit for a king. As a Christian representing our Lord, how important do you feel it is to be dressed appropriately for the occasion?

3. Dressed in her royal robes of authority and power, Esther knew it was time to approach the king. Where was the king?

Esther knew that no one was allowed to present himself or herself to the king without being summoned, not even the queen. She had not seen him for 30 days. To appear before the king unsummoned was what assassins tried to do, and because of such a threat whoever came without permission into the presence of the king was immediately put to death.

4. Apparently the king was proceeding with the affairs of the kingdom of Persia when Esther crossed the threshold of the royal court into his presence uninvited. Describe the king's reaction when he saw Esther.

> [After] he held out his golden scepter to her as proof that her life was safe, Esther knew the first part of her prayer had been answered. Her life was spared. She had not prayed for wisdom in vain. . . . She sensed that this was neither the time nor the place for her urgent request. Her insight into this situation reveals she was a wise woman in control of her emotions and one who didn't need to make hasty decisions. She was also a woman who realized very practically that the way to a man's heart is often through his stomach. She invited the king to a meal—along with Haman."[1]

5. How did Proverbs possibly give Esther encouragement?

   Proverbs 22:11

   Proverbs 25:15

6. How did the king respond to Esther's invitation to a banquet (verse 5)?

7. What was Esther's answer when the king asked again, *Now what is your petition?* (verse 6).

Esther's judgment was equal to her courage. She proceeded cautiously one step at a time, waiting wisely, sensing it was not yet God's time for her to ask for the salvation of her people. Perhaps the inner voiceless voice of God had warned her, *Do not state your request tonight—wait until tomorrow night.*

God wanted the king to base his decision on more than the love he felt for Esther. He needed to understand there was much more involved than an emotional decision. There were certain facts that he needed to comprehend. In chapter 6 we will see how those facts are made clear to him.

MEMORY CHALLENGE

Record Galatians 6:9.

DAY SIX

Gallows of Rage

Read Esther 5:9-14.

1. Haman left the palace happy and jubilant over having been included in the banquet with the king and queen. What happened at the palace gate that angered him?

Lesser people exaggerate slights, while the great can afford to overlook them. Haman was a man obsessed, driven by his need for approval, forgetting his elevated position of power. Mordecai was only a judge at the king's gate. Haman was the prime minister.

2. There is nothing that soothes wounded egos more than sympathetic listeners. As his wife and friends listened, Haman recounted to them all that made him proud. List all that Haman bragged about.

Promoted by the king, honored by the queen, and advised by his wife and his friends, Haman seemed to have life at its best.

3. From Psalm 37 list some blessings of those who trust in the Lord.

   What does this psalm tell us about the future for the wicked Hamans who turn against God and His people?

   Human pride can lead to rash actions and reactions. Could Haman have been encouraged to have been a better man if his wife and friends had been godly, giving him wise counsel instead of revengeful advice?

4. How was Haman advised to punish Mordecai for his disobedience?

First Samuel 25 records the influence of another wife coping with her evil husband. Unlike Zeresh, Abigail was praised for wisdom as she considered Nabal, her arrogant and overbearing husband.

Nabal owned large areas of land and was a successful sheep owner. While David was hiding from Saul in the wilderness of Paran, Nabal gave a feast for his sheep shearers. David and his 600 men were camped near the town of Maon. He heard about Nabal's feast and requested some food. This was the custom of those times; David's men had been good to Nabal's sheepherders and had been like a wall of protection around them day and night (1 Samuel 25:15-16).

Nabal refused the request and pretended not to know of David. In his anger, David determined to kill Nabal's entire household. Nabal's wife, Abigail, anticipated David's reaction and loaded a convoy of donkeys with food to feed all of David's men. When David met Abigail he was impressed with her beauty, humility, praise, and advice (1 Samuel 25:32-35).

5. Read 1 Samuel 25. How did David respond to Abigail's request not to shed blood to avenge himself and his men (see verse 35)?

To be responsible for our family is a priority in our walk with the Lord. Our care of them and counsel to them must be done considering God's Word and His instructions in each situation. We can be a Zeresh, agreeing with and encouraging retaliation and revengeful reactions; or we can be an Abigail, taking great effort to restore peace. She was willing to be used to protect her loved ones in a difficult and dangerous intervention and involvement. God gives wisdom as we live in His Word and receive discernment and guidance from His Holy Spirit.

At the suggestion of Zeresh, Haman's wife, and all his friends, Haman ordered the workmen to construct in his own courtyard (7:9) a gallows, 75 feet tall in order that it could be seen from afar, probably even from the palace.

Construction began that very night because Haman was overly confident that the king would grant his request. He would make an example of this impertinent Jew, Mordecai, and this would enable him to enjoy Esther's second banquet with complete peace of mind. Instead, it turned out to be his very own place of death.

Esther's purpose in inviting the king and Haman to a private banquet was to accuse Haman of plotting to destroy her people. Providentially, she postponed her request and invited them to another banquet the following evening. This decision demonstrates the basic meaning of the Book of Esther: unfailing providence of God on behalf of His people, Israel.

MEMORY CHALLENGE

Write out Galatians 6:7-9 from memory.

Wisdom of the Word **Bible Study Series**

Esther

■ **A study of Esther 6—7**

DAY ONE

Sleepless in the Palace

Read Esther 6:1-2.

1. That night the king could not __________.

   That night after Queen Esther had entered the inner court of the king's palace and the king had granted permission for her to be in his presence;

   That night after he and Haman had accepted Esther's invitation and attended the banquet she had prepared for them;

   That night after Esther had not revealed her request when he had two times offered her half his kingdom if that was her request;

   That night after Esther had asked that he and Haman accept a second invitation to another banquet she would prepare for them the next day;

   That night on which his prime minister, Haman, had devised a scheme to rid himself once and for all of Mordecai, the Jew;

   That night when gallows were being constructed on which to kill Mordecai Haman had no doubt that the king would go along with his evil plan. The king did not hesitate to consent for the extermination of the whole Jewish race. What would cause him to intervene on behalf of one Jew who was an influential troublemaker?

   That night the king's insomnia changed the course of history for the Jews.

2. Daniel 6:16-18 tells of another king who was sleepless in his palace. What kept King Darius from sleeping?

3. From Proverbs 21:1 explain how kings can be directed by the Lord.

4. Although God is all-powerful and all-knowing, how has He chosen to let us help Him?

   1 Timothy 2:1-2

   James 5:16

MEMORY CHALLENGE

Galatians 6:10

As we have opportunity, let us do good to all people, especially to those who belong to the family of believers.

5. Unable to sleep, how did King Xerxes choose to spend the hours of the night?

Records carefully preserved in the royal archives were read to the king. Judging from the account of Mordecai we previously read (Esther 2:21-23), this was not dull reading. As the king reviewed the history of his reign, he was reminded of a time when Mordecai was responsible for saving his life by furnishing information causing the arrest and execution of the king's would-be assassins.

Although King Xerxes continued to be deceived in knowing the true character of Haman, *that night* he was made aware of the truth about Mordecai—he was the king's friend. He had risked his life to save the king from assassination.

There were gallows beside Haman's home (7:9). Haman planned for it to be used in the 24 hours between the two banquets. Who was going to hang?

Chapter 6 of Esther begins with a restless and sleepless king, which seems an uneventful incident. Yet it's amazing how natural occurrences can form important parts of momentous events. A review gives timely importance to day-to-day events:

2:7 Esther is adopted by Mordecai, a devout Jew

1:19 Vashti is removed as queen.

2:17 Esther is chosen as queen.

2:22 Mordecai overhears and reports an assassination scheme.

4:16 Esther is willing to appear uninvited before the king.

5:4 Esther shows wisdom in making her request to the king

5:5 The king agrees to attend the banquet.

6:1 The king has a sleepless night and reads records.

The king's sleepless night in the palace began his change of heart towards the Jews. A holy God was working His plan, in His way, in His timing, for His people.

You must believe that God is working on your behalf today. He has been working quietly and consistently throughout your lifetime. God is always at work. He is in sovereign control over the course of your life if you love Him and are living according to His purpose.

6. Record Romans 8:28.

God works in "all things"—not just isolated incidents—for our good. This does not mean that all that happens to us is good. Evil is prevalent in our fallen world, but God is able to turn every circumstance around for our long-range good. Notice that God is not working to make us happy, but to fulfill His purpose. Notice also that the promise is not for everybody. It can be claimed only by those who love God and are called according to His purpose. Those who are "called" are those the Holy Spirit convinces and enables to receive Christ. Such people have a new perspective, a new mind-set on life. They trust in God, not in life's treasures; they look for their security in heaven, not on earth; they learn to accept, not resent, pain and persecution because God is with them.[1]

DAY TWO

Prideful in the Palace

Read Esther 6:3-9.

Two men were making plans for Mordecai:

1. King Xerxes had been reminded that he owed his life to Mordecai. The discovery of this forgotten act moved the king greatly. From verse 3 explain the king's response to this reminder.

2. Haman had arrived early in the outer court of the palace eager to speak to the king about Mordecai. How did his request differ from the king's thoughts at that time?

The king's intentions were to honor. Haman's intentions were to destroy.

Learning from the historical record of his reign that nothing had been done to honor Mordecai for saving his life, the king decided that a reward with honor was long overdue. Seeking appropriate suggestions for proceeding with his plan, he asked for an available member of the court to be brought to him.

Could it have been that Haman too might have had a sleepless night? In his scheme to murder Mordecai, he arrived at the outer court very early, hoping to obtain the king's permission to complete his evil plan to hang Mordecai on the gallows he had erected near his home (7:9).

It is generally agreed by many commentators that Haman still had the confidence of the king and that the king and Haman did not know of Mordecai's relation to Esther.

3. As you read the passage of 6:6-9, what are your thoughts of Haman?

Completely deluded by his egotistical opinion of himself and believing the king would be delighted to honor *him*, Haman answered quickly with his suggestions of what should be done *for the man the king delights to honor* (verse 9).

4. It is interesting that Haman knows very well how to honor someone. Could he have remembered the honoring of Joseph by Pharaoh? From Genesis 41:41-43, describe how Joseph was dressed and how he was honored.

   How does your answer compare with Haman's suggestions for honoring someone?

Pride is easier to recognize than to define, easier to recognize in others than in oneself. To value a child, a parent, a friend, a job well done—to value your country, to be patriotic, and so on—is the positive, healthy side to pride. But the Bible looks primarily at the destructive side of pride so that we can identify those areas of our character that are displeasing to God. We can then bring them before Him, asking Him to cleanse us from these sins.

Haman was already a man with power and authority, but he was obsessed with prestige. He did not suggest giving the honored man great wealth, because he craved public acclaim—popularity and recognition. Haman was proud and arrogant. He was presumptuous in believing the king would honor him. He was self-centered and boastful.

Pride is the opposite of humility, the proper attitude one should have in relation to God. Pride is rebellion against God, because it attributes to self the honor and glory due to God alone. It leads to a hardness of heart, which in turn leads to an arrogant disregard of God and sin.

Prayerfully write out Psalm 139:23-24.

MEMORY CHALLENGE

To whom should we do good?

DAY THREE

Mordecai Honored

Read Esther 6:10-13.

1. Believing that he was *the man the king delights to honor*, what shocking command did Haman receive from the king?

2. What was Haman's response?

Broken and humiliated, Haman obediently carried out the command of the king, *proclaiming before him, "This is what is done for the man the king delights to honor!"* —the words that Haman had expected to be proclaimed for himself.

Haman's plans were in complete reversal! Haman was giving honor to the troublesome Mordecai, who had not given honor to Haman—who saw himself equal to King Xerxes.

God was true to His promise to care for His chosen ones. Mordecai would surely recognize that although he was never rewarded for his act of saving the king's life, God had been waiting for the right time. Just as Mordecai was about to be murdered unjustly, the king realized he should honor this one who had served him courageously.

There are times in our lives, through no fault of our own, when we are serving the Lord as we understand He is leading us, that we find ourselves being misunderstood and persecuted. As we remain faithful and true to His Word, we will see His intervention in our behalf—in His way, in His time, for our good and His glory.

3. In your opinion, why does God sometimes not intervene until the gallows are erected?

4. Record the following promises:

   Isaiah 54:17

   2 Corinthians 2:14

   Galatians 6:9

The parade was over. Although Mordecai had been given recognition and honor by the king, his position in the court of the palace had not changed. He humbly and unassumingly returned to his accustomed station at *the king's gate.*

5. From 6:12 describe Haman's departure from honoring Mordecai.

   From 2 Samuel 15:30, name another who covered his head as a sign of great personal grief and despair.

6. Again, Haman explains the events of his day with his wife, Zeresh, and his friends (6:12-13). How is the mood of this gathering different from that of the previous time they met together (5:10-14)?

7. The friends mentioned in this passage (and in 5:10 and 5:14) had previously advised him to take vengeance upon Mordecai. With Zeresh and the advisers apparently just learning that Mordecai was a Jew, what gloomy prediction was made to Haman by his wife and advisers?

Haman received no encouragement at home. Zeresh predicted his downfall. His advisers were probably those who, by casting lots, had chosen the day the Jews were to be destroyed. Also, they were the ones who had suggested erecting the gallows. Now that they know Mordecai is a Jew and has been honored by King Xerxes, they see only ruin coming to Haman. Are their words showing an abandonment of Haman? They said "you" or "your" three times in their comments to him. They're walking away from having any responsibility for his downfall.

How has the ungodly pride and arrogance in Haman's character led to his humiliation? "Pride leads the fool to experience shame. Thus, Haman's excessive pride led him to propose an ostentatious ceremony to honor someone who turned out to be his enemy. His own prideful words led to his shameful exaltation of Mordecai."[1]

8. Humility versus pride:

Psalm 18:27—*You save the* ___________ *but bring low those whose eyes are* ___________.

Proverbs 11:2—*When* __________ *comes, then comes disgrace, but with* ___________ *comes wisdom.*

Proverbs 13:10—___________ *only breeds quarrels.*

Proverbs 15:33—___________ *comes before honor.*

Proverbs 16:5—*The Lord detests all the* _________ *of heart. Be sure of this: They will not go unpunished.*

Proverbs 16:18—_________ *goes before destruction, a haughty spirit before a fall.*

Proverbs 18:12—*Before his downfall a man's heart is* __________, *but* _____________ *comes before honor.*

Proverbs 29:23—*A man's* _________ *brings him low, but a man of* _________ _________ *gains honor.*

Jeremiah 49:16—*The* _________ *of your heart [has] deceived you.*

Matthew 23:12—*Whoever exalts himself will be* ___________, *and whoever* ___________ *himself will be exalted.*

9. What is one weak part of your character you would like to be more Christlike?

How have you seen negative consequences of this weakness?

With God's help, what is one way you will determine to be stronger in this weakness?

MEMORY CHALLENGE

Name three ways we can do good to people.

DAY FOUR

A Time to Speak

Read Esther 6:14—7:4.

With predictions from his advisers and his wife that *you will surely come to ruin*, Haman was hurried away to the second banquet that Esther had prepared.

1. Record the guest list of those invited to the banquet.

2. Again we read the king's gracious consideration of Esther. What was his question?

3. This was Esther's time to express her request to the king. Her silence had been appropriate, but the time had come for her to speak. Record phrases from the following passages that relate to Esther's wisdom:

   Proverbs 10:19

   Proverbs 17:27-28

   Ecclesiastes 3:7

James 1:19

The king had already questioned Esther two other times: in the throne room when she first approached him and he welcomed her by holding out his scepter, and again at Esther's first banquet. But Esther had never answered him, because the time was not right. Esther knew when to act, and she knew when to wait. She had never told the king she was Jewish, and she waited for the right moment to break her silence.

4. From 7:3 name those that Esther specifically mentioned in her request to the king.

5. What words from 7:4 reveal how Haman wanted the Jewish population totally removed from Persia?

   How do these words compare to the language of the royal decree written by Haman (3:13)?

Designed only to satisfy his evil pride, Haman had convinced the king that the decree would be in Persia's best interest. If he could destroy the influence of Mordecai and all other Jews, he would remove any threat to his own ability to exploit the kingdom for his own wicked benefit.

The Jewish people were referred to in Deuteronomy as the apple of God's eye (Deuteronomy 32:10). No one could harm His chosen ones without risking His wrath (Zechariah 2:8-9)—not even a king. So it was not just the lives of Esther and her people who were in danger—the welfare of the king was a concern. For King Xerxes there would be suffering far greater than losing the Jews as his servants and much worse than the hatred that would occur against him with such a decree—the king would be turning against God. Therefore, Esther wanted to protect the king also.

When Queen Esther revealed her request, both the king and Haman were shocked, because neither of them knew her nationality. She now identified herself with her people. Haman and the king began to grasp the impact of the decree they had dispatched throughout Persia: the queen and her people were scheduled to die. The king was hearing his queen plead for her life. He must have seen clearly that this was the reason she dared approach him uninvited. No doubt he was angered and alarmed at the thought that her life was in danger.

Earlier on this day, a prideful, angry, and bitter Haman had been forced by the king to honor Mordecai—and now he discovered that the queen was one of the people he planned to destroy, and she was related to this archenemy, Mordecai. Haman must have been a very troubled and frightened guest as the banquet continued.

We must admire the courage and wisdom of Esther in the timely and graciously effective presentation of her request. Her insight and approach resulted in the king's respect and succeeded in convincing him that she was telling him the truth regarding Haman and the decree.

O Lord, unlike Esther, too often we run ahead or procrastinate too long in making decisions and acting on them. Today make us aware of a time to be silent or a time to speak; a time to be still or a time to act. We want to radically obey You.

MEMORY CHALLENGE

How were Esther and Mordecai good to those who belong to the family of believers?

DAY FIVE

Do Not Be Deceived

Read Esther 7:5-7.

1. In a word picture, describe Haman as you see him when Esther identified him as the one who wanted all Jews annihilated from Persia.

2. In your opinion, why was the king in a rage?

   Explain the reason for the king's anger described in 1:12.

   From Genesis 39:13-19 explain why another deceived leader reacted in anger.

> To deceive is to cover up the truth, the facts, to make things seem different from the way they really are. To deceive is to send someone in the wrong direction. Even telling only half the truth is a form of deception because it is manipulating information to get your way. What makes deception so bad is that it is not just a mistake or an oversight; it is a calculated plan to mislead another, a deliberate attempt to get someone to believe an untruth. Deception breaks the bond of trust that is so necessary to human relationships. God hates deception because He not only stands for truth, He is the embodiment of truth. He will never deceive, and His truth will never lead you astray. . . . If someone is trying to convince you to believe something that contradicts Scripture, you can be assured it is wrong. . . . As long as Satan has power to deceive, he will deceive others, and they in turn will deceive us. The worst kind of deceiver is the false teacher, who appears to come for our good, only to lead us on a destructive path.[1]

3. With lies and flattery the king had been deceived. Christians must guard against being deceived. Record phrases from the following passages:

   How can Christians be deceived?
   Romans 16:17-18

   Colossians 2:4

   2 Thessalonians 2:1-3

   What agents of deceit are working to defeat us?
   Romans 7:11

   2 Corinthians 11:14

   James 1:22

   1 John 4:1

   How do the wicked practice their deceit?
   Psalm 35:20

Jeremiah 9:8

Romans 1:29-32

2 Timothy 3:12-13

King Xerxes had believed that Haman was planning for the king's and Persia's best interest. He had placed authority in Haman that reflected the confidence and trust that he had in him. He had been naively unaware of the plot that had developed in his own court and that he had so casually approved. He had failed to see any connection between Esther and the unnamed people whose destruction he was allowing (3:13) until Esther revealed the truth to him.

Conflicting emotions must have raced through his mind. He had learned

- His queen would be a victim of the decree he had authorized. She was a Jew.
- He had not seen Haman as the man he was and had elevated him to the highest-ranking position of his kingdom. He had been manipulated into agreeing to Haman's evil scheme, and the seal from his signet ring had given the authority that would see Haman's evil bloodbath put into force.

4. *The king got up in a rage, left his wine and went out into the palace garden* (7:7). As you think of the king in the garden, probably considering what action he should take concerning Haman, record the phrase from Esther 1:6 that you choose as the most striking feature of the garden.

While the king was in the garden, Haman was begging Esther for mercy, realizing she was his only hope not to be killed by the king. Earlier in the day, he had been ordered to lead the Jew he hated, Mordecai, in a triumphal procession through the streets of Susa, and now he was pleading with a Jew for his very life.

The true character of each of those involved in this passage is clearly seen:

Haman—An arrogant braggart becomes a whining coward when his deceitful and evil plans are exposed to the king.

Xerxes—Unpredictable and easily deceived by flattery, he is shown to be weak despite his place of power.

Esther—The queen had been informed by wise Mordecai of exactly what was happening in the Persian kingdom. She boldly proceeded to save her people. She was victorious through the courageous and wise presentation of her request to the king by faithfully following the concepts of Jewish wisdom.

Unlike Haman, Esther did not stir up the king's anger but appeased it. She did not rush into the king's presence with her request but waited patiently. She chose just the right time to speak and then did so with a *gentle tongue* (Proverbs 25:15). She chose her words carefully. She did not mention that she was Jewish.

We continue to see God moving behind the scenes in the Book of Esther. God watches over His own. No weapon formed against Israel will prosper. God blesses those who bless the Jews and curses those who curse the Jews —and Haman had been cursing them.

Father, many warnings from Your Word advise that as Your coming draws nearer, we must guard against deceiving spirits as Satan goes over the world seeking those he can kill and destroy. Alert us to the Hamans and the Hitlers who proclaim lies that are presented as truth. We trust You to defeat any weapon formed against us.

MEMORY CHALLENGE

Record Galatians 6:10.

DAY SIX

Rewards and Punishment

Read Esther 7:8—10:3

Visualize this scene: the king returned from the garden and he saw Haman half fallen on the queen's couch. (Haman had broken a very strict rule of court etiquette. To approach the queen and speak to her without the king present was to cause great offense.) Down on his knees, he was desperately pleading for mercy, seeking the queen's intervention on his behalf. The sight of this offended and disgusted the king. Accusingly he said, *Will he even molest the queen while she is with me in the house?* Notice the horror of the scene for Haman—his attempt to beg for mercy had failed miserably.

1. What action did the attendants of the king take?

2. What had caused the same thing to happen in 6:12?

3. Harbona was one of the seven eunuchs whom the king had sent to bring Vashti to the great banquet (1:10) In Harbona's reference to the gallows (7:9), how was Mordecai identified?

4. Following the suggestions of his advisers, as usual, and being reminded of Haman's true character and knowing of the evil plot against his friend Mordecai, how was the angry king's fury subsided?

5. We all get angry at times. What should we do about our anger?

   Matthew 5:21-26

   1 Corinthians 13:5

   Ephesians 4:26-27

Haman died on the very gallows that he had built for hanging innocent Mordecai. This is an illustration of the belief of Jewish wisdom that those who do evil will be punished by the work of their own hands.

6. In the following passages, summarize how Jewish wisdom predicts not only the end of Haman but also the success of Esther and the rescue of Mordecai:

   Proverbs 11:19

   Proverbs 12:13

   Proverbs 14:35

   Proverbs 16:14

Proverbs 21:8

Proverbs 26:27

In chapter 6 we read that Haman believed he would be honored, and now he is put to death. In chapter 4 we see that Esther believed she might die, but now she will be honored.

The success of Esther, in contrast to the failure of Haman, established her as wise and righteous. She was an example of one who waited for the proper moment to speak and to say no more than was necessary. Proverbs 17:27 says, *He who has knowledge spares his words, And a man of understanding is of a calm spirit* (NKJV). Being in control of her remarks, Esther said no more than was necessary to accomplish convincing the king of the desperate situation of the Jewish people. Reflecting proverbial wisdom, Esther stated her request confidently, clearly, and carefully.

7. As we prayerfully allow the Holy Spirit to guide us, God will help us to know when to speak, how to speak, and when to remain quiet. Have you had an experience when God helped you in this way? If comfortable, share this with others to encourage them.

In this passage we have seen justice being carried out. The wicked have been punished, and the righteous have been rewarded. Does this always happen in your experience? When you choose to do what is right, are you always rewarded? Are your good choices always the right ones, or have some of your situations become worse because of your choices?

Today it seems the wicked are prospering and causing havoc for Christians. Righteous people are suffering and being persecuted and murdered. One day that will change. *The righteous man is rescued from trouble, and it comes on the wicked instead* (Proverbs 11:8).

- Pharaoh had the Jewish boy babies drowned (Exodus 1:22), and God drowned his army in the Red Sea (Exodus 14:28).
- Daniel was delivered from the lion's den, and the people who accused him took his place and were slain (Daniel 6).
- Peter was delivered from prison, and his guards were executed (Acts 12).

Our motivation for being obedient and doing what is right is to please God. We believe that justice will ultimately occur because of God's promises. We may not witness justice in this life, but we know from Scripture that justice will be done.

8. How do you agree with Psalm 73:1-16?

List phrases from Psalm 73:16-28 that give you comfort, hope, and assurance.

When we're disappointed and questioning the lack of justice, we must go to God and His Word for His perspective. We must continue to do what is right whether or not we witness justice happening now.

MEMORY CHALLENGE

Quote Galatians 6:7-10 from memory.

Esther

■ A study of Esther 8—10

LESSON 5

DAY ONE

Rewards for Goodness

Read Esther 8:1-2.

1. How is Haman identified?

2. From Proverbs 22:22-23 explain the Lord's warning to those who mistreat others.

   Explain how this concept of justice proved true for

   Esther

   Mordecai

The king could take the property of Haman and give it to Esther because the government had the authority to confiscate the estate of condemned criminals. With Esther's disclosure of her relationship with Mordecai, he then became one of the privileged few with access to the king's presence. With his promotion by the gift of the royal signet ring from the king and the appointment by Esther to manage her estate, Mordecai was rewarded with all the prestige, authority, and wealth that Haman had known.

3. According to the following passages, what brings rewards from God?

   Psalm 18:22-24

   Proverbs 19:17

   Proverbs 25:21-22

   Jeremiah 17:10

MEMORY CHALLENGE

Proverbs 3:5

Trust in the LORD with all your heart and lean not on your own understanding.

Matthew 5:11-12

1 Corinthians 3:5-9

James 1:12

Being offended by Mordecai's refusal to bow before him, Haman learned that hatred and bitterness are very dangerous emotions that usually turn against the one who unleashes them.

4. How do the following verses instruct us about offenses?

   Proverbs 17:9

   Proverbs 18:19

   Proverbs 19:11

We do not want to offend or be offended. It is painful. We know that when we "cover over" an offense it promotes love and harmony, and it is for our good and God's glory. But there are times when we're so offended that the pain and injustice overwhelms us. We know we must forgive and not be bitter, but instead we find our hearts turning away from forgiveness toward bitterness and even begin to have a desire for revenge. We experience discouragement and shame. Our lack of forgiveness causes us to see ourselves as spiritual failures.

5. What do the following passages teach us about unforgiveness?

   Leviticus 19:17-18

   Proverbs 14:21

   Proverbs 24:17

   Matthew 18:21-22

After reading these truths, we may determine to be forgiving, but there's a major problem—with the beginning of the process of forgiveness, unexpectedly the anger and injustice returns. Our peace of mind is eroded, and we're again robbed of joy. We see as never before that we must recover from our bitterness because of what it does to us. We cry out to be healed of our pain, to be freed from our anger, and to be comforted in our grief so that we can leave this problem behind us and move on in our lives.

Marty was in the heartache of such a painful struggle. A relationship that was very important to her had unexpectedly experienced a divisive misunderstanding. She had learned that choosing to forgive was only a small part of what she needed to do. Forgiveness was proving to be an emotionally costly struggle. It was a continuing process —not instantaneous. The Matthew 18:21-22 passage helped to show her that she must forgive over and over and over. Her continued effort to forgive was in obedience to God's Word and her desire to be like Jesus in whom she had received forgiveness.

Marty's counselor had advised her that often deliverance is necessary when those involved will not cooperate to come to a peaceful solution. After a particularly difficult conversation, she cried out to God as never before, *Dear God, help me. Show me what's wrong with me. I'm so sick and tired of being a failure for You.* In that gentle voiceless voice of the Holy Spirit she heard, *Marty, you can live above this.* All the pain of failure, guilt, and unrest left her. The light of the Holy Spirit flooded her heart, and the darkness of misunderstanding and defeat left her. God answered her cry with a deliverance from the torment of this attack from evil.

6. Have you had an experience of forgiving that you could share that might encourage someone else?

7. Do you need others to pray with you to give you encouragement or guidance in a difficult struggle?

DAY TWO

Faithfulness of God

Read Esther 8:3-14.

Esther had exposed the enemy, and Haman was dead, but his decree to destroy the Jews had not died. It had been written, sealed with the king's signet ring, and delivered throughout the kingdom.

1. From Esther 8:3-4, explain Esther's actions as she began to plead for her people.

2. From verse 5 list the phrases that reflect an oriental custom Esther used preceding her request of the king.

Dramatically falling at the king's feet and using phrases of humility, Esther implied that Haman, not the king, was responsible for the decree ordering the death of her people.

3. Summarize the king's responses to Esther's request (verses 7-9).

4. (Optional) From Daniel 6, explain how another king was distressed over a law of the Medes and Persians.

The king continued his hands-off style of leadership by trusting Esther and Mordecai, just as he once trusted Haman. Haman's decree, sent out in the king's name, could not be annulled, but a second decree could be issued to counteract it by allowing the Jews to be prepared to defend themselves by anticipating the attack on the appointed day. The king gave permission for Mordecai to prepare this second decree, which would counteract the first without actually canceling it.

Mordecai's decree included four main defensive acts:

1. The Jews were to gather into groups by the 13th of Adar.
2. They were to defend their lives and the lives of their families.
3. They were to kill those who attacked them.
4. They were to take the property of their attackers.

Only by knowing of the second decree and responding to it could the terrible slaughter of the first decree be avoided. Mordecai's emphasis was on self-defense against the attacking Medes and Persians, not aggression against innocent people.

5. What special emphasis is placed upon the speed with which Mordecai's decrees were sent out, in comparison to that of Haman's decrees in 3:13?

6. Mordecai's list of those receiving the second decree had an addition (8:9) that had not been included in the list of those receiving Haman's decree (3:12). Who had been added?

A little over two months after the first decree was issued by Haman, the official letters by Mordecai were prepared and sent throughout the empire. The Jews had eight to nine months to prepare their defenses.

Couriers on royal horses delivered the new decree throughout the empire, including the capital of Susa (8:14).

The Book of Esther proves that God is faithful. He provides and cares for His people. In these last chapters of Esther we see that God brings justice in His time and in His way. Sometimes the justice comes in the way we expect, and at other times we're caught by surprise by God's ways. From an overwhelming opposition of our Hamans to the smallest concern of our every day, God continues to be faithful.

7. From the following passages write a thought or phrase that describes the faithfulness of God.

   God's faithfulness is
   Infinite—Psalm 36:5

   Established—Psalm 89:2

   Unequaled—Psalm 89:8

   Unfailing—Psalm 89:32-33

   Everlasting—Psalm 119:90

   Great—Lamentations 3:23

   God's faithfulness is manifested in
   His covenant-keeping—Deuteronomy 7:9

   His promises—1 Kings 8:20

   His statutes—Psalm 119:138

   His judgments—Jeremiah 51:29

   His plans—Isaiah 25:1

   His forgiveness of sins—1 John 1:9

8. Describe a time when God proved himself faithful to you in a difficult situation.

9. How are you faithful to God while you're waiting for Him to act in your life?

Father, just as You were faithful to Mordecai, Esther, and the Jews, You are faithful to me. Please remind me when I am being unfaithful to You.

MEMORY CHALLENGE

Trust in the LORD with _______ your ________ and _______ _______ on your own _____________.

Proverbs 3:5

DAY THREE

God Honors Fasting

Read Esther 8:15-17.

After having issued the second decree, Mordecai left the king's presence clothed in the regal garments of blue and white, the royal colors of Persia. A crown of gold and a robe of purple linen completed his royal attire.

1. If Mordecai had thought back to a few weeks before, how would he have remembered being clothed (4:1)?

2. What was the reaction of the city of Susa to the new decree (8:15)?

3. What had been the reaction of Susa to the decree of Haman (3:15)?

4. What was the response of the Jews to God's provision and protection (8:15-17)?

5. How did the response of Mordecai, Esther, and all the Jews to the first decree (4:1-3, 15-16) prepare the way for the events of chapter 8?

Beginning with her request for all the Jews to fast for her (4:16), Esther became transformed, from the passive and obedient wife of Xerxes and daughter of Mordecai to one who took charge and gave directions to save her people. Mordecai, by contrast, no longer gave instructions to Esther but became obedient to her. Through their cooperation with God, the Jewish population was saved.

Many more instances of fasting are recorded in Scripture. Every area of our lives would receive benefit from this neglected discipline.

Fasting is defined as abstaining from physical nourishment. From each of the following passages, record a phrase about fasting:

A. Occasions of fasting:

Personal requests—1 Samuel 1:7, 17, 20

National repentance—1 Samuel 7:5-6

National grief—Nehemiah 1:3-4

Personal loss—2 Samuel 12:15-17, 22-23

Alarming danger—Esther 4:16

Anxiety—Daniel 6:18-20

Sacred ordination—Acts 13:2-4

B. Fasting can be accompanied by

Sorrow and confession—Nehemiah 9:1-2

Mourning—Joel 2:12-13

Prayer—Luke 2:36-37

C. Safeguards concerning fasting:

Endure scorn—Psalm 69:9-12

Learn the true meaning of fasting—Isaiah 58:6

Fasting must not be a ritual without remembering God— Zechariah 7:5-6

Avoid display—Matthew 6:16-18

D. Results of fasting:

Divine guidance—Judges 20:26-28

Victory over temptation—Matthew 4:1-11

Margretta Bundy believes strongly in the discipline of fasting:

> From the time that I first felt the presence of the Holy Spirit in my life as a very young child, I had a burden for the salvation of my father. I truly loved and respected him, for, you see, he was my daddy.
>
> Many revivals came and went at our home church, and always there was a tearful child who whispered to her so-gentle father, "Daddy, don't you want to go to the altar tonight?" His answer was always the same: "No, not tonight, little darlin'."
>
> My dad, who was a wonderful man with character, had a sinful habit that he knew stood in the way of him honestly trusting his life to Christ. The blessing that I will always be grateful for is that he continued to attend church and place his tithe in the offering plate every Sunday.
>
> When I was a senior in college, our Acapella Choir was preparing music for our choir tour. We had one week to finish this preparation. During this week I asked precious friends in the choir to please join me in prayer for my daddy, for I knew he was planning to meet me at our final performance to take me home for the summer. I spent this week in much prayer and fasting for his salvation. I was not hungry. Food was not appealing to me. I just couldn't eat. I could drink water. God had called me to fast.
>
> When we reached our destination, my dad was there. My prayer was that God would speak to him during the wonderful service. I did not want to go to him with the same invitation that I'd whispered to him so many times in my life. I wanted my Lord to do the inviting. Oh, my, how hard it was for me to stand still and not leave the choir and go to my daddy! I clung to a friend's skirt—so determined to keep my position in the choir. She whispered, "Margretta, you're about to pull my skirt off."
>
> I then looked up and saw my father running to the altar. Something placed my one foot after the other as I ran to meet him there.
>
> Many gathered around him while his precious head was bowed to the floor. He confessed so sweetly, and God answered. I praise Him for answered prayer in the salvation of my daddy.

Be sensitive to the urging of the Holy Spirit. If He requires fasting to answer your petitions, you will not be alone. He will strengthen you for what He calls you to do.

When our prayers are answered, we can do as the Jews did (9:17) and celebrate with joy.

MEMORY CHALLENGE

We may not fully understand fasting, so when we trust in the Lord, we do not lean on our own _____________.

DAY FOUR

Triumph of the Jews

Read Esther 9:1-17.

In the Introduction to Esther at the beginning of this study, we read, "This is a dramatic and rather gory tale of love, hate, and palace intrigue." Chapter nine includes the gory portion of the story of Esther; but it also tells of the providential triumph of the Jews over their enemies. The purpose of the writer in recording these events is fulfilled in this chapter. On the day the king had commanded for his decree to be carried out, the Jews gathered together in their cities throughout all the provinces of King Xerxes.

1. Why were their enemies unable to stand against the Jews?

2. What was the unexpected reaction of all the leaders in the empire?

The rulers had to choose between two conflicting decrees. They chose to support the one issued by the man who was now in power.

3. After reviewing 3:13; 8:11; 9:10, 15, 16, explain how the Jews treated the property of those they killed.

The Jews refrained from taking advantage of their rightful privilege and opportunity to confiscate the property of those they killed. They wanted it known that they were fighting for their very lives and that their motive was not for material gain from their enemies. Esther 9:5 suggests that the Jews were free from any intervention from the king's officials, but they acted in self-defense, attacking those who sought to kill them.

4. There is no mention of Haman's 10 sons until 9:7-10. How did they share in their father's guilt?

5. What was Esther's request regarding Haman's sons, who had been killed?

Scripture does not explain Esther's motive for having Haman's sons on display on the gallows. Most commentaries suggest that the sight of the 10 bodies would serve as a warning to others who might have attacked the Jews. Before judging Esther too harshly for her decision, we must remember that the Jews in the Old Testament period did not have the light we have on moral issues. In many books of the Old Testament, we find instances of apparent cruelty on the part of the Jews (Judges and 1 Samuel).

Esther dared to risk death for her people, and this resulted in her escaping death as well. She was a genuine patriot and in the hour of crisis was not ashamed to confess being a part of her Jewish race.

Our own nation, state, and community need godly patriots, as Esther was needed so many years ago. Christians should *shine like stars in the universe* (Philippians 2:15). Esther was such a "star"—which is the meaning of her name.

Your life situation is not like Esther's. God has placed you in your own environment, and there are unparalleled opportunities of serving God and a needy world. Serve the Lord to the limit of your availability where in His providence He has placed you, and you will be preparing yourself for a larger area of service, if it is His will for you.

Through Esther God has shown that His guidance is available to His followers for making decisions.

6. From the following passages record phrases about making your decisions.

   My decisions should be
   - Based on the Word of God—John 14:21
   - Tested by prayer—James 1:5
   - Confirmed by the counsel of others—Proverbs 15:22
   - Dependent upon an inner assurance—1 John 3:21
   - Made possible through God-opened doors—Revelation 3:7-8

We cannot imagine such a cruel slaughter of people. Only under circumstances to save our nation and the lives of our loved ones would Christians consider taking the life of anyone, and this was the consideration of Mordecai, Esther, and her people.

Dear Father, protect our nation from evil.

MEMORY CHALLENGE

Have you learned to trust in the Lord with all your heart?

DAY FIVE

Purim Celebrated

Read Esther 9:18-32.

Mordecai sent out another letter (9:20).

1. Who received the letter?

   Explain the purpose of the letter.

2. What were these days of celebration called?

   Why did these days have this name?

3. How did the Jews respond to Mordecai's letter (9:27-28)?

4. In verses 29-32, a second letter about Purim is sent. Who wrote this letter?

   What was the purpose of the second letter?

In regard to the Jews observance of Purim, Charles Swindoll writes,

> This reminds me of the spontaneous celebration that became the first Thanksgiving in the New World. After enduring the bitterness of winter, the early colonists decided to hold a feast, celebrating their survival and giving thanks to God for His protection and

provisions throughout the past months. It was a spontaneous celebration of praise. It was our forbears' Purim. God had turned their hardship and sorrow and pain into gratitude and health and joy. This early feast officially became Thanksgiving when the governor of Massachusetts declared it so.[1]

From the first celebration of Purim *(purim* is the plural form of *pur)*, it has never been known as a Jewish holy day, but it has enjoyed great popularity among the Jews. Its popularity may be due to the fact that it is the only secular holiday on the Jewish calendar for the celebration of the lighthearted side of life.

The 13th day of Adar is kept as a day of fasting in remembrance of Esther's fast before she spoke to Xerxes. In the evening, which is the beginning of the 14th day, Jews assemble in their synagogues. After the evening service, the reading of the Book of Esther is begun. Everyone cheers the hero and heroine (Mordecai and Esther). When the name of Haman is reached, the congregation cries out, "Let his name be blotted out," or "The name of the wicked shall rot." They boo and hiss and stomp their feet. The names of Haman's sons are all read in a breath, to indicate they were hanged simultaneously. It is not uncommon for Haman to be hung in effigy and to use noisemakers with rattlers to celebrate this.

The next morning the people gather again at the synagogue and finish the religious services of the festival. They then devote their day to happy rejoicing before the Lord. Besides sharing of food, they give gifts to the needy.

Purim is not a reenactment of a tragedy; it is a celebration of triumph. It is a celebration of deliverance. Unlike Hanukkah, another festival of deliverance in which the achievement of religious liberty is celebrated and the preservation of Israel remembered, Purim commemorates the preservation of the Jewish people. The story of Esther is a symbol, as Purim is a symbol, of the deliverance of the Jews. The nation and the people are spared. This is not an isolated event but is typical of Israel's history; as the people have been persecuted time and again, so they have often been delivered. The festival of Purim is a constant reminder year after year that though persecution may come to the Jews, deliverance is certain. They believe that though all the prophetic books may be forgotten, Esther will always be remembered; Purim will always be observed.

What does the Book of Esther mean to Christians? We can't answer this question without appreciating what it means to Jews. To the Jew it has been stated in one phrase: "The indestructibility of Israel." Israel will be preserved because it is God's plan. This is not clearly stated in Esther; there is no mention there of God and His purpose, but there can be no doubt of the providential development of His designed plan.

We read Esther as we read the parables. Jews have been persecuted—there has been a Haman, a Hitler. Jews have been delivered—there has been a Mordecai and an Esther, the allied forces of World War II. If not these names, then we have others—those of the people who fight anti-Semitism, of those whose loyalty to Israel is without limit.

We as people of God must never forget the warning of Genesis 12:3—*I will bless those who bless you [the Jews], and whoever curses you [the Jews] I will curse.*

MEMORY CHALLENGE

How do you lean not on your own understanding?

DAY SIX

God's Divine Providence

Read Esther 10.

1. List phrases from 10:3 that describe Mordecai.

Mordecai did not let his place of power, as second to the king, keep him from sincerely promoting the peace and welfare of his people. Because he remained their friend, he enjoyed a good reputation among the Jews. In contrast to Mordecai's life, we see in Haman's life the worthlessness and emptiness of superstition as a guide to life. God, not the throw of dice *(pur)*, controls the destinies of men. The plan through which God works is His divine providence—His wise guidance of people and circumstances.

2. From each passage, what phrase describes God's providence?

   It has a purpose—Genesis 45:5-8

   It is mysterious—Job 11:7-9

   It is universal—Psalm 103:19

   It is all-powerful—Psalm 115:3

   It is righteous—Psalm 145:17

3. List a phrase showing how God's providence is manifested in the world.

   It will continue—Genesis 8:22

   It orders humanity's life—Psalm 75:6-7

   It provides—Psalm 104:27-28

   It controls the smallest details—Matthew 10:29-30

   It guides the world—Acts 17:26-27

4. List phrases that instruct us as believers as to how we should acknowledge God's divine providence:

   1 Chronicles 29:11-12

   Psalm 37:3-7

Psalm 139:10

Proverbs 3:5-6

How can believers trust God's divine providence in adversity, in their struggles?

Job 1:21-22

Psalm 119:75

Hebrews 12:5-6

Too often we don't recognize God's providence until we look back on our yesterdays, but when we look back we can see that God was there.

Esther has taught us that God has a plan for every life. When Esther understood her responsibility, she was transformed from a pampered queen to one of the great heroines of all times. God has a purpose for every life. For that purpose He has brought you to this particular place, time, and opportunity.

5. Summarize what Jeremiah 29:11-13 says to you:

This is a powerful and encouraging promise. If you're thinking your life does not count for anything, that your life has no purpose or meaning—be of good courage! If you're radically obedient, if you're trusting in Him with all your heart, if you're serving Him as you understand your responsibility—even if it's in the small things of obedience—then you're fulfilling His will for your life.

God sacrificed His Son that you may have eternal life with Him in heaven—and on earth. Living eternal life on earth with Him is filled with His divine providence. Let Him master your life with His love and forgiveness. Look with joyful anticipation as you live for Him each day. In His divine providence, He changes us from glory to glory—and the day will come when we will see Him face-to-face.

MEMORY CHALLENGE

If we believe in God's divine providence, we can quote Proverbs 3:5 with full assurance.

Introduction to Ruth

The Book of Ruth is a short historical narrative considered to be one of the most beautiful pieces of literature in the Bible. In contrast to most biblical narratives, it is a story of a private family rather than of national or international affairs. It involves family relationships with husbands, wives, children, in-laws, and relatives. It shows the role each family member plays in filling the needs of other members of the family and the family as a whole. The story moves smoothly from famine, dislocation, and death in Moab to a happy ending in Bethlehem with the harvest seasons, marriage, and the birth of Obed, the father of Jesse and grandfather of David.

Naomi, Ruth, and Boaz show great loyalty and faithfulness in their commitment to God, family, and community. Naomi was concerned for the welfare of her widowed daughters-in-law, although she had no legal obligation to them. Ruth's loyalty and faithfulness to Naomi went beyond cultural expectations as did her obedience to Naomi in seeking marriage with Boaz, the family protector. It emphasized her commitment to family.

Boaz showed consistent faithfulness and family loyalty when he accepted the double responsibility of purchasing the land and marrying Ruth, which allowed the preservation of the lineage and inheritance of Elimelech's family, which otherwise would have ended with that generation.

According to the law of the levirate marriage (Deuteronomy 25:5-10), if one brother died without having a son, the next brother was to take the widow and provide an heir for his dead brother. In the case of Ruth, who had no brothers-in-law, a more distant relative could marry her. A relative was the only one who had the right to redeem the inheritance of a dead person, and yet he was under no obligation to do so. The willing, generous response of Boaz was, in a very small way, a foreshadowing of our Great Redeemer, who was to descend through him. This family line was preserved not by wives of patriarchs but by an elderly widow and her non-Israelite daughter-in-law. As ancestors of David, the most famous king in all Hebrew history, Ruth and Boaz became ancestors of Jesus Christ (Matthew 1:5, 16).

Ruth

■ A study of Ruth 1—2

DAY ONE

Naomi Grieves

Read Ruth 1, focusing on 1:1-5.

1. When did the story of Ruth take place?

The time of the judges was the period between the death of Joshua until the reign of Saul. (Optional: read Judges 2:6-19.)

2. Record the following:

The last sentence of Judges 2:19

Judges 17:6

3. What was the condition of the land of Israel at the beginning of the story of Ruth?

Why was the land in this condition (Deuteronomy 11:16-17)?

4. What did Elimelech do to try to provide for his family?

5. From Ruth 1:3-5 list all that happened to Elimelech and his family during their years in Moab.

6. From Joshua 23:6-8, 12-13 explain how the Israelites had been instructed to live with the heathen nations.

MEMORY CHALLENGE

Job 19:25

I know that my Redeemer lives,
and that in the end he will stand upon the earth.

Disobeying God's laws given by Joshua, Elimelech had taken his family to live in the heathen nation of Moab. After Elimelech's death, his sons had also disobeyed God's laws by marrying women of Moab. Moabites were descendants of Lot (Genesis 19:30-38), making them distantly related to the Jews. But instead of worshiping God, the Moabites were idolaters. Their god, Chemosh, was worshiped through the sacrifice of children as burnt offerings. (Optional: read 2 Kings 3:26-27.)

7. From Ruth 1:3-5 list three or four words that you would use to describe Naomi's life in Moab.

The Book of Ruth presents a contrast to the tumultuous events described in the Book of Judges. We read of the joys and sorrows of a godly family, God's providential leading, and the fulfillment of His plan to bring forth His Son.

Living among heathens who worshiped pagan gods and suffering the loss of her husband and her sons, Naomi was in difficult and sad circumstances. There was almost nothing worse than being a widow in the ancient world. Widows were taken advantage of or completely ignored. Naomi not only had her own grief to suffer but also was concerned for her daughters-in-law. The natural order of life is marriage, children, grandchildren, and perhaps even great-grandchildren, and then death. It had not happened that way for Naomi. Parents shouldn't have to bury their children, but Naomi did. Twice.

Specialists report that friends, relatives, and clergy can never underestimate the extent of the pain that parents experience when a child dies. Couples who experience the death of a child tend to have high divorce and suicide rates. The grief and the healing process contain the same elements for all bereaved parents. But for those whose adult children have died, additional factors affect their grief, experts say. There are many more memories—both good and bad. People often assume that because the child was an adult, the pain of loss is less. The grief of parents after the death of an adult child is often discounted.

With permission from the national office of the Chicago-based organization Compassionate Friends, we are giving their recommendations for helping those who have lost children. These could also be applied to the loss of a spouse or other loved one.

> The death of any child overwhelms the parents regardless of the cause of death or the child's age. Parental grief is intense, long lasting and complex. Families are more likely to reach a healthy, positive resolution of their grief if they receive support and understanding. The following suggestions may help you provide that support:
>
> - Don't try to find magic words that will take away the pain. There are none. A hug, a touch and a simple "I am so sorry" offer real comfort.
> - Don't be afraid to cry. Your tears are a tribute.
> - Avoid saying, "It was God's will," and other common phrases that attempt to minimize or explain the death.
> - Avoid saying, "I know how you feel." It is very difficult to comprehend the depth of the loss when a child dies, and to say you do may seem presumptuous to the parents.
> - Listen. Let them express their anger, the questions, the pain, the disbelief and the guilt they may be experiencing.
> - Avoid judgments of any kind. Decisions and behaviors related to displaying or removing photographs, reliving the death, idealizing the child, or expressing anger, depression or guilt may seem extreme in many cases. These behavior patterns are normal, particularly in the first years following the child's death.
> - Be aware that, for the parents with religious convictions, their child's death may raise serious questions about God's role in this event.
> - Be there. Run errands, help with household chores, provide childcare and help in whatever way is needed.
> - Give special attention to surviving children. They are hurt, confused and often ignored. Don't assume they are not hurting because they do not express their feelings.
> - Mention the name of the child [or spouse] who has died. Don't fear that talking about the child will cause the parents additional pain. The opposite is usually true.
> - Be patient. Understand that grieving families respond differently to their pain.

James 1:27—"External religious worship [religion as it is expressed in outward acts] that is pure and unblemished in the sight of God the Father is this: to visit and help and care for the orphans and widows in their affliction and need, and to keep oneself unspotted and uncontaminated from the world" (AMP.).

We need to be available for those suffering losses in their families. When you know people who are grieving, ask God to give you the words and deeds that would comfort them. We can be a ray of light in their sadness.

DAY TWO

Letting Go

Read Ruth 1:6-14.

1. Explain the changes being made in the lives of Naomi, Ruth, and Orpah (verses 6-7).

2. What was Naomi's hope for her daughters-in-law?

3. Why might the words spoken in verses 8-9 have been difficult for Naomi to say?

   Why was it important for her to say them?

4. What are some ways that family members or friends can let go but still express love?

5. Can you share an experience of letting go while you were able to continue expressing love and caring?

6. As you name each member of your family, consider prayerfully whether you ought to reach out to him or her more or to let go more.

7. Prayerfully personalize the first phrase of each of the following scriptures:

   Proverbs 17:17

   Romans 12:9

   Ephesians 5:2

   1 Thessalonians 3:12

Although Naomi lived among a heathen population for over 10 years, she never forgot the God of her fathers. Being an Israelite, she longed to be with her family and those who believed in the God of her people. As a widow, she was dependent on the kindness of others. Without her husband and sons, she needed her relatives and friends. After hearing that the famine was over in Judah and that the Lord had visited the people there by giving them food, Naomi wanted to go home. She wanted to return to Bethlehem of Judah, her homeland.

Like Naomi, Virginia, too, had lost her son. After grieving her loss, she had to let go of her hopes and dreams for James, her only son. His children, Phil and Jan, became Virginia's greatest concern. After time to accept his dad's death, Phil continued his education and today is a successful Christian businessman. Jan had a very different reaction to her dad's death. She questioned God's lack of protection of her godly, kind, and gentle dad. She bitterly turned her back on God and began a chaotic lifestyle of rebellion. In time she was a member of a cult, had two children out of wedlock, and lived a life isolated from her family for years.

Virginia had to let go of Jan. She gave her complete acceptance without any expectations. When Virginia died, Jan gave a tribute to the unconditional love of her grandmother. She told that after her dad died, she felt that the God all her family knew was not a God she ever wanted to know. She expressed this to her grandmother and was not scolded or rejected. Instead, was held, loved, and encouraged. Virginia pledged her love and support of Jan and asked her to keep in touch with her. She assured Jan that she would pray for her throughout every day and that she would always be available for her in all circumstances.

During her years of rebellion Jan would receive letters from Virginia every week. She would receive gifts for her birthday, Easter, Thanksgiving, Christmas, Mother's Day and many other times of the year—always with the assurance of her grandmother's love and prayers. At the end of her tribute, Jan held up a well-worn Bible that Virginia had mailed to her when Jan's life was at its worst. She tearfully said, "The Lord is my shepherd because the Bible and my grandmother told me so."

Today Jan is a single mom and a highly respected schoolteacher, giving credit for her accomplishment to the unconditional love of her God and her grandmother. God so faithfully honored Virginia's letting-go of her granddaughter and trusting God to be with her.

In submission to her husband, Naomi had let go of her home in Bethlehem. Now he and her two sons were gone, and she longed for her former home. Our first home is one that we must let go of as we leave to make our own home. And yet we always carry our first home with us. It would be wonderful if we could think of that home and feel loved, cherished and accepted just as we are, with all our frailty, fears, and flaws; a home where we didn't have to be perfect to be loved, a home with forgiveness when we didn't deserve it. Many of us haven't had this kind of home, but we have seen or experienced enough of those moments to know it's possible. It's an ideal we can work toward to unconditionally love each other and be quick to give forgiveness when it's needed to improve our relationships in our homes. He wants peace and harmony in our lives. He is our Helper!

Heartbroken and disappointed, Naomi made the decision to return to Bethlehem. Her consistent faithfulness while living in Moab influenced both Orpah and Ruth for good. When Naomi was ready to return to Bethlehem, her daughters-in-law began the trip to Judah with her. Knowing that Ruth and Orpah would be giving up their homeland, their relationship with family and friends and their chance to marry men of their own country, Naomi chose to let go of the girls and let them be free of any responsibility toward her.

Consider the times you have let go. There are those times for all of us when we had no choice and painfully released circumstances that we wanted to keep. It was heartbreaking, and our lives were disrupted. Then there are other instances when we let go because we made a choice that it was for the best. Or we may have felt directed by God and were obedient. God rewards the obedience of letting go. Abraham was willing to let go of his son, Isaac, as a sacrifice, and God sent a substitute (Genesis 22); Hannah let go of Samuel, and he became a prophet of God (1 Samuel 3); Mary let go of her son, Jesus (John 19), and now we can have eternal life through Him; the father let go of his prodigal son, and he returned home (Luke 15). We must not be afraid to let go.

MEMORY CHALLENGE

I know that my Redeemer __________, and that in the end he will stand upon the earth.

Job 19:25

DAY THREE

Naomi—A Mentor

Read Ruth 1:14-18.

Record phrases answering the following questions:

1. How did Ruth convince Naomi to stop telling her to return to Moab?

2. Where was Ruth going?

3. Where would Ruth live?

4. Would Ruth have a family in Bethlehem?

5. Ruth was breaking free from the idolatry in Moab. Why was she forsaking Baal and Chemosh?

6. How did Ruth express that her decision was permanent?

7. What strong oath of assurance of her commitment to Naomi did Ruth declare?

8. How did Naomi react when she was convinced that Ruth wasn't returning to Moab?

The Chaldee paraphrase that follows relates the debate between Naomi and Ruth:

> Ruth said, "Entreat me not to leave thee, for I will be a proselyte."
>
> Naomi said, "We are commanded to a Sabbath-day's journey."
>
> "Well," said Ruth, "whither thou goest I will go."
>
> Naomi said, "We keep Sabbaths and good days, on which we may not travel above 2000 cubits and are commanded not to tarry all night with Gentiles."
>
> "Well," said Ruth, "where thou lodgest I will lodge."
>
> Naomi said, "We are commanded to keep 613 precepts."
>
> "Well," said Ruth, "whatever thy people keep I will keep, for they shall be my people."
>
> Naomi said, "We are forbidden to worship any strange god."
>
> "Well," said Ruth, "thy God shall be my God."
>
> Naomi said, "We have four sorts of deaths for malefactors: stoning, burning, strangling, and slaying with the sword."
>
> "Well," said Ruth, "where thou diest I will die."
>
> "We have," said Naomi "houses of sepulcher."
>
> "And there," said Ruth, "will I be buried."[1]

How did Naomi gain such loyalty from two foreign daughters-in-law? She must have been concerned when both of her sons had chosen Moabite women to marry. She knew the Law of Moses prohibited a Moabite from entering into the congregation "of the Lord even . . . to the tenth generation" (Deuteronomy 23:3). God had specifically warned against intermarriage with foreign nations. He knew they would turn their families away from serving Him (Deuteronomy 7:4).

In spite of her sons' disobedience, Naomi not only accepted Orpah and Ruth but also truly loved them. They obviously felt her love and loved her in return.

According to the oriental custom, when Mahlon and Chilion married, they brought Orpah and Ruth to live in the home of their mother. Naomi, the older woman, was in charge of the household and responsible for relationships within the home. As a foreigner in Moab, Naomi would have had habits, customs, and beliefs different from those of her daughters-in-law. Naomi became a mentor to the wives of her sons as they became a part of the Hebrew home.

9. Summarize Titus 2:3-5.

All of us have had mentoring in our lives. Some of the most effective mentors are parents, grandparents, aunts, uncles, cousins, friends, teachers, and neighbors.

What is involved in being a mentor? Webster defines a mentor as "a trusted counselor and guide." A mentor is a teacher and encourager who shares his or her knowledge about life, builds up self-confidence, and gives emotional support. A mentor shares freely from his or her life, speaking of failures as well as successes, helping younger men and women learn from their experiences.

Young adults need older men and women to teach important roles in life: how to be an adult, nurture their children, nurture themselves, and love their mates. Mentors in the workplace are needed to help others be more successful. As I use my computer, I could use someone younger to be a mentor for me today!

One of the greatest learning experiences of my life was in mentoring young mothers while I was adjusting, not too well, to the empty nest syndrome. We studied God's truths. We became accountable to one another in applying His truths to our everyday lives. We exchanged what we had learned in caring for babies and coping with toddlers. We laughed together and cried together. We ate together and exchanged recipes. We prayed for our husbands—some of them were still attending college, some were establishing businesses, and some were beginning professional careers. We prayed for one another—for depression, illness, unexpected pregnancy, miscarriage, lack of money, problems in relationships, loss of a parent or grandparent, and especially for spiritual growth and direction.

As these honest and sincere needs and solutions were shared, I learned insights into my daughters' lives that I could not have been taught any other way. I needed the input of this group of mothers, as they needed mine. They helped me to be young at heart while they filled my life with deeper meaning and purpose. Young adults can have the appearance of having it all together, but many struggle with inferiority, loneliness, self-doubt, rejection, abuse, weariness, and fears for the future. Orpah and Ruth would have had some of these feelings as they became a part of Naomi's family. Their caring for Naomi and their willingness to leave their homeland to move to Judah with her show that Naomi's support, wisdom, love, and commitment to them was returned with their love and loyalty.

10. Can you share with others an experience when a mentor helped you? Is God showing you that He wants you to seek a mentor for a need in your life? Is God placing a desire in your heart to be a mentor?

Father, as my God and Guide, You can bring into my life those I need to help me. I open my heart for Your direction. You are the Almighty Master of all You have created, and that includes me. I trust You!

MEMORY CHALLENGE

I know ______ ____ ____________ ________, and that in the end he will stand upon the earth.

Job 19:25

DAY FOUR

In Bethlehem

Read Ruth 1:19-22.

Naomi and Ruth had arrived in Bethlehem after climbing the desolate trail that followed a ridge of mountains through the Judean wilderness. They had carried what they could of their belongings and had arrived exhausted from the trip.

1. What was the response of the town to Naomi and Ruth?

It wasn't just a relative or friend who was surprised at the arrival of Naomi and Ruth, but the whole town was shocked. The citizens of the city saw Naomi aged, wrinkled, and dressed in widow's attire. She had only a Moabite woman as a companion. The appearance of poverty and stress were very evident. Naomi, who had formerly been well to do, was now obviously in want.

2. Visiting with the townspeople stirred up feelings in Naomi. Explain how you interpret her attitudes at this time:
   - toward herself
   - toward the Lord
   - toward Ruth

Naomi's loss of her husband and sons overwhelmed her anew as she met relatives and friends and acquaintances of her hometown. Grief is unpredictable and often comes when we don't expect it. Naomi reacted by speaking harsh feelings of bitterness and self-pity.

Naomi's words were out of character for the kind and gentle spirit she had shown in her difficult years in Moab. In this moment of self-pity, Naomi's lack of concern for Ruth was seen when she called herself "empty" when loyal Ruth stood patiently at her side. Sometimes blinded by grief and filled with self-pity, we're enveloped as in a house of mirrors, seeing only ourselves and not considering others. As we continue the study of Ruth and Naomi, we will see Naomi again become the wise and loving mentor to her daughter-in-law.

As painful as life can be when we suffer brokenness, God often uses brokenness to bring us to obedience. In Naomi's case, her heart was broken, and then in the distressing circumstances of widowhood her will was broken, which caused her to return to Bethlehem.

3. From the following scriptures explain the importance of Bethlehem:

   a. 1 Samuel 16:1, 13

      Matthew 1:5-6, 16-17

   b. Micah 5:2

      Matthew 2:1

      John 7:42

Their move to Bethlehem wasn't just to benefit their living conditions, but it played a vital role in the fulfillment of prophecy of the birth of Jesus Christ.

God disciplines with brokenness. He breaks people's emotional hearts as a means of getting them to give Him their spiritual hearts. Naomi had been through years of the discipline of brokenness before she left the heathen land of Moab and returned to Judah.

4. Record the following scriptures:

   Job 5:17

   Psalm 94:12

   Scan Hebrews 12:5-10, and summarize verse 10.

5. From the following passages summarize experiences of brokenness:

   Daniel 4:23-37

   Luke 15:11-24

6. Can you share an experience of brokenness (physical, emotional, or financial) that God used to move a person toward accepting Jesus Christ as Savior?

MEMORY CHALLENGE

I know that my Redeemer lives. If He is not your Redeemer today, confess your sins to Him, ask Him to forgive you, and invite Him into your heart. He will accept you, and all of heaven will rejoice.

DAY FIVE

Ruth

Read Ruth 2, focusing on verses 1-13.

Ruth meets Boaz, and their love story begins.

1. Refer back to Ruth 1:22 and explain what is taking place in the grain fields of Judah.

2. Summarize 2:2-3.

Ruth was the new girl in town. She was a foreigner, a Moabite. She willingly assumed the role of provider for Naomi and herself. She knew of the Hebrew law that ordered landowners not to harvest in the corners or edges of their grainfields. Grain that was dropped was to be left for needy people (Leviticus 23:22). Because Naomi and Ruth were widows with no source of income, they were eligible for this type of welfare program in Israel.

Ruth was a stranger and a foreigner in Bethlehem, and her reputation was yet to be determined. She was like a blank page that was ready to be filled out.

3. Scan 2:1-13 and list the attributes of Ruth that Boaz would discover as he studied her.

   List the character qualities of Boaz that Ruth could see in forming her opinion of him.

4. Is there a character quality of Ruth or Boaz that you would like to develop in yourself? When would be the best time to begin?

Ruth had taken the initiative to ask Naomi's permission to begin searching for food. She didn't let it be defeating to her that she was a foreigner in a land that didn't approve of her. She didn't bask in self-pity for what had happened to her in the past. Ruth saw what needed to be done and did it. Her fears of rejection and retaliation did not let her become a prisoner inside of four walls. She stepped outside her home and did what needed to be done, one step at a time and one day at a time.

We can't always fix feelings. We can't turn them on or off as we choose. Like the weather, they can change without notice. Ruth might have felt anxious, scared, rejected, or needy. It's all right to have feelings as long as these feelings don't control us and keep us from doing what needs to be done. Ruth had a purpose—to provide for Naomi and herself. To have a purpose and a goal stabilizes us, and when we forge ahead, although it is difficult, it often results in improved feelings as we see ourselves successful in our endeavors.

As Ruth and Boaz are considering each other, their opinions will come from more than verbal communication. Ninety percent of our information is from nonverbal cues. Facial expressions, body movements, tone of voice, eye contact, and empathy can reflect warmth, friendliness, and acceptance.

As Boaz learned more about Ruth, what was his opinion of her? In the gleaning of barley from his field he saw her industriousness, perseverance, courage, bravery, humility, and her obedience to his instructions. In her care of Naomi she was thoughtful, dependable, responsible, sacrificial, authentic, devoted, and hard-working. She possessed an inner core of confidence and determination to fulfill her responsibility to care for Naomi. Ruth was not just a fair-weather friend.

5. Summarize Ruth 2:12.

Boaz was expressing a blessing over Ruth.

6. Name the characteristic of God in each of the following verses:

   Exodus 19:4

   Psalm 36:7

Psalm 57:1

Psalm 91:4

Ruth had found a place of refuge in Israel's God. As a hen gathers her young under her wings to protect them from harm, so God protects those who come to Him for safety.

7. Can you encourage others by sharing a time when you felt protected and loved by God?

MEMORY CHALLENGE

I know that my Redeemer lives, and that in the end ____

______ ________ ________ ____ ________.

Job 19:25

DAY SIX

Boaz

Read Ruth 2, focusing on verses 13-23.

Boaz's remarks to Ruth were unexpected, and she responded with humility and gratefulness. She regarded herself as inferior to the girls who worked for Boaz. Because of her status as a widow, her poverty, her Gentile nationality, and her heathen background, she didn't expect his kindness toward her.

Boaz continued to give her generous and kind considerations throughout the day.

The Book of Ruth is a prophetic revelation of the nation of Israel. The nation of Israel, like Naomi, is on her way back to her ancient land. (The state of Israel was established May 15, 1948, and many Jews have returned to their homeland since then.) The marriage of the Church (that's us), foreshadowed by Ruth, will take place when the Lord Jesus, the Bridegroom, foreshadowed by Boaz, will shout from the air, and we will rise to meet Him (1 Thessalonians 4:16-17).

1. Boaz noticed Ruth and inquired about her just after his morning greeting of blessing to his workers. When did Christ take notice of you?

   Ephesians 1:4

   2 Timothy 1:9

2. Boaz knew about Ruth's leaving her family and homeland to come to Bethlehem to care for Naomi. What does Christ know about you?

   John 2:25

   Hebrews 4:13

3. Boaz gave instructions to help Ruth as she gleaned. What instructions does Christ give to you?

   Matthew 11:28

   John 5:24

4. Boaz made special provisions for Ruth. What special provisions has Jesus made for you?

   John 14:1-3

   John 14:16-18

   John 14:27

   John 15:11

   John 16:23-24

   John 17:15

   Romans 5:9

   2 Peter 1:3

5. Boaz desired that God would bless, reward, and protect Ruth. What is Christ's desire for your life?

   Ephesians 3:16-21

6. Consider Boaz's care of Ruth. How does this help you to see Christ's love for you?

God is working in our lives in ways we may not recognize. Events in our lives do not occur by luck or coincidence. Ruth didn't accidentally or by chance decide to go to the field of Boaz to glean for barley. God's guidance had been with her from the moment she began her search until she stepped onto the property of Boaz. As we go through our everyday lives, we can trust that in God's providence He is directing our lives for His purpose.

MEMORY CHALLENGE

Quote Job 19:25 from memory.

Wisdom of the Word **Bible Study Series**

Ruth

■ A study of Ruth 3—4

DAY ONE

Naomi Makes Plans

Read Ruth 3, focusing on Ruth 3:1-4.

1. As Ruth continued gleaning through the barley and the wheat harvests, where was she living? (Ruth 2:23)

2. What do you consider as Naomi's motivation for finding Ruth a secure home?

3. Widows in the time of Naomi and Ruth were as needy as the street people of today. The only place they could find safety and respect was in the home of a husband. Without a kinsman-redeemer willing to take responsibility for them, their future was very bleak. Scripture does not tell us how Boaz was related to Ruth's deceased husband, but the nearest male relative could assume the responsibility of marrying a relative's widow. Assuming a parental role, Naomi presented a plan to her daughter-in-law that would make it possible for Ruth to become the wife of a kinsman-redeemer.

   List each step of her plan (3:3-4).

The harvest in the fields of Bethlehem had come to an end, and now it was time for threshing and winnowing the grain. The threshing floor, where the grain was separated from the harvested barley or wheat, was made of rock or hardened soil and usually was located out in an open area to make maximum use of the breeze. "The grain stalks were crushed either by hand or by oxen, and the valuable grain (the inner kernel) was separated from the worthless chaff (the outside shell)."[1] In the late afternoon, when the breeze had picked up after the day's heat, the threshed grain was tossed into the air (or winnowed) by using a pronged fork on a long handle. The breeze blew the lighter chaff a short distance away (later gathered to be used to feed their animals), while the grain fell back to the threshing floor. At the end of the harvest, after the grain had been winnowed and the winds had subsided, about midnight, an elaborate meal of celebration was served. Then it was time for a night of rest and sleep. The owner of the grain would spend the night beside the heap of winnowed grain to guard it against thieves who would otherwise steal it.

As each day of the harvest had gone by, Ruth enjoyed the favor of Boaz as she continued gleaning in his grain fields. He went far beyond any legal responsibility as a landowner to a gleaner working in his fields. Naomi saw romance developing without any steps toward marriage being taken. So she came up with a plan. Three things stood in the way of marriage for Boaz and Ruth:

1. Boaz was not the nearest of kin.
2. Naomi held the first right of marriage to the legal kinsman-redeemer. She must show she waived her legal claim in favor of Ruth.

MEMORY CHALLENGE

Job 19:27

I myself will see Him with my own eyes—
I, and not another. How my heart yearns within me!

3. Boaz knew he was not the nearest kinsman. He didn't know that Ruth would prefer him, an older man.

Naomi knew that if Ruth would follow her plan, all of these problems would be overcome.

Naomi's plan was proper according to the customs of those times. Ruth would not be claiming a favor only for herself. She would be claiming a right for her dead husband and his family. Gleaners had to go to the landowner and claim their right to glean. Likewise, a widow could go to the kinsman and claim her right of marriage. Naomi knew Boaz would lie down among the heaps of grain. He would cover himself with his all-purpose cloak that served as a blanket by night. Ruth's uncovering his feet would symbolize her claim on him for marriage.

Naomi was familiar with the routine of the harvest and the threshing of grain. She gave Ruth explicit instructions for her personal appearance and the timing to approach the place where Boaz would be sleeping. Ruth had been dressing appropriately in her widow's attire. Now she was to lay aside this reminder of her unhappy time in Moab. She was now free to meet a potential husband, so she put on a beautiful robe.

Ruth had risked humiliation when, dressed in working clothes, she had asked to glean in the field of Boaz. This second request involved risk also. Instead of just grain for daily food, she would lay claim to Boaz's whole estate and personal life. She risked great humiliation if Boaz refused the responsibility of kinsman-redeemer.

Without Naomi's loving advice, how could Ruth ever have gone to Boaz in this way? It was a very daring plan, but she trusted Naomi and knew her mother-in-law wanted her to have a good life. She respected the older woman's knowledge of customs, as well as her sensitivity, common sense, and wisdom.

4. While we are considering the possibility of Boaz and Ruth's engagement to be married, can you share an experience of someone's engagement?

DAY TWO

Obedience Can Be Tough

Read Ruth 3:5-9.

1. Summarize the following verses:

   Ruth 3:5-6, explaining Ruth's response to her mother-in-law's instructions

   Colossians 3:20

2. Boaz went over to the heap of grain to sleep after he had finished eating and drinking. According to Naomi's instructions, Ruth quietly went to where Boaz was sleeping and uncovered his feet and lay down. Summarize the following verses:

   Ruth 3:8-9

   Ezekiel 16:8

3. Describe a time when obedience was difficult for you.

4. What was Christ's attitude toward obedience?

   Matthew 26:39 (last phrase)

   Philippians 2:8

   Ephesians 5:21-29

   Ephesians 6:2

We have seen or been an active participant in ministering tough love. Genuine love demands toughness in time of crisis. There must be defined limits for people of all ages. Smothering love reinforces irresponsibility and generates disrespect. By making it clear that there are limits to what will be tolerated, self-respect and confidence grow.

Ruth's obedience to follow Naomi's instructions may have been tough obedience for Ruth. Obedience is always the result of faith, of believing the promises of God to the extent that we act on them. Tough obedience is to obey when it demands daring, courage, boldness, and risk of failure with rejection and humiliation. Although she had gleaned in the grain fields of Boaz for both the barley and wheat harvests and had received special favor from him, she was aware of her foreign nationality, which was despised by the Jews. She felt she *[did] not have the standing of one of [his] servant girls* (2:13). Would Boaz want to fulfill the role of kinsman-redeemer to a woman of Moab? How would an older, wealthy Jew respond to her?

Ruth was to keep hidden until the end of the harvest celebration was over. She would wait until all sources of light had been extinguished and the threshing floor was quiet from any activity. She was to wait alone and in hiding until Boaz was asleep. She would then walk softly to where he was sleeping, uncover his feet, and lie down. Ruth accepted Naomi's advice and fulfilled the bold and daring plan. When Boaz realized there was a woman at his feet, he did not ask her what she wanted—he knew what she wanted. His question to her was *Who are you?*

5. As you read the following passages, list phrases that would require tough obedience:

   Romans 13:1, 7

It is tough obedience to submit to one another. It can be especially challenging in a marriage in which it is largely opposites who have attracted one another. The special traits that were so appealing in dating can become strong irritants after a few months of marriage. With a strong commitment to marriage and compromising in many areas, the blessing of mutual submission will bring a marriage of peace and contentment. Without mutual submission there can be no harmony. (There are some abuses that go beyond what anyone should be expected to endure, however. God would not expect submission to an abusive husband or wife.)

It is tough obedience for a son or daughter to honor an abusive parent. To honor is to show respect with mannerly behavior. A son of an abusive father requests prayer from his Christian friends and family any time God directs him to visit his father. He spends as much time as he can without reacting to his father's abusive words—in the beginning it was only 10 minutes—and then he leaves. He gives God all the credit for answering the prayers of those he has contacted to agree with him in prayer during his visits.

It is tough obedience to submit to authority that is not honorable. Where there is selfish ambition at the cost of integrity, only in obedience to God can we be submissive to dishonorable leaders. Knowing that God honors obedience, we can trust Him to fulfill His promises to us. *If my people, who are called by my name, will humble themselves [obey His word] and pray and seek my face and turn from their wicked ways, then will I hear from heaven and will forgive their sin and will heal their land* (2 Chronicles 7:14).

It is tough obedience to forgive the devastating betrayal of a friend or family member. To be like Jesus we must be able to say, *Father, forgive them, for they do not know what they are doing* (Luke 23:34).

It is tough obedience when we are doing all the right things for the right reasons and feel that God is far away. Again we must look to Jesus as our example: *My God, my God, why have you forsaken me?* (Matthew 27:46). He has promised never to leave us or forsake us, but He does allow testing times that make us stronger in Him.

6. Can you share an experience of tough obedience that later brought blessings to you?

To refuse to obey diminishes our fruitfulness. Jesus tells us in John 15:1-2, *I am the true vine, and my Father is the gardener . . . every branch that does bears fruit he prunes so that it will be even more fruitful.* Tough obedience is one form of God's pruning.

Pruning is God's way of removing more of self-centeredness from our lives. Tough obedience is difficult because more of self must die. To submit to one another removes more of our pride and releases our need to control. To respect abusive parents humbles us. To submit to dishonorable authority takes faith in God alone to believe that through our obedience He will bless our nation and us. Pruning is God's way of making the priority of our lives to seek first His kingdom and His righteousness (Matthew 6:33). Tough obedience is based on these principles:

1. There is no reason that we cannot obey God, or He would not expect it.
2. We cannot complain or tell Him it doesn't make sense.
3. We cannot compromise His commands or be in denial that God would expect this of us.

We can determinedly begin to obey when it is tough; then we will experience the peace, joy, and comfort of our abiding in Him, with Him abiding in us.

MEMORY CHALLENGE

Who will see God with their own eyes?

DAY THREE

Sitting at the Feet of Jesus

Read Ruth 3:10-14.

1. From Ruth 3:10 we know that Ruth's action received Boaz's approval. What was the earlier kindness that Boaz referred to? (Refer to Ruth 1:16-17; 2:2.)

Boaz showed pleasure that Ruth had chosen him rather than a younger man. A woman is drawn to a man who provides loving leadership, plus Ruth had witnessed his relationship with other people. He was considerate of his employees and relatives. He showed special kindness and generosity to Ruth because he was aware of her care of Naomi.

2. What did the men in town think of Ruth?

Record the following scriptures:
Proverbs 12:4 (first phrase)

Proverbs 31:10

3. Summarize Deuteronomy 25:5-6.

Due to the death of Ruth's husband, someone needed to inherit the land and continue his family's name. "A tradition states that Boaz was 80 years old when he married Ruth. . . . Boaz was only a nephew of Elimelech, [Ruth's deceased father-in-law], whereas a brother was still living. . . . Boaz insisted on allowing the man with the closest relationship to decide whether or not he wished to assume the responsibilities. . . . He would be a protector responsible to redeem property that had been alienated."[1]

4. If Ruth was to become Boaz's wife, who would be her husband when they all spend eternity in heaven (Matthew 22:24-30)?

5. Why would it be important to Boaz and Ruth that it not be known that Ruth spent the night with Boaz? Refer to the following scriptures:

   Romans 14:16

   2 Corinthians 8:21

Our reputation is made by those who know us. A good reputation comes by consistently living our beliefs before those who see us at home, at work, in our everyday activities—at the store, the gym, involvements at church, and in every other area of our lives.

6. Why is it important to have a good reputation?

7. While lying at the feet of Boaz, Ruth received his blessing: *The Lord bless you, my daughter.* What do we learn from the following passages about coming to the feet of Jesus, our Redeemer?

   Luke 7:36-50 (a sinful woman). Record Jesus' words from verses 48 and 50.

   Luke 8:40-42, 49-56 (Jairus). Record Jesus' words from verse 50.

   Luke 10:38-42 (Mary). Summarize verses 41-42.

   Luke 17:11-19 (the thankful leper). Record verse 19.

At the feet of Jesus, as we speak our love to Him, our sins can be forgiven. As we make our requests to Him in faith, the dead can be revived. As we express our frustrations to Him, He can gently correct us. And as we give Him our thanks, He can heal us.

8. In your own words, from the following passages express why it is important to "come to the feet of Jesus" with our requests:

   Psalm 10:17

   Isaiah 57:15

   James 4:10

If you know the following hymn, sing it to your Heavenly Father:

Sitting at the feet of Jesus,
Oh, what words I hear Him say!
Happy place! so near, so precious!
May it find me there each day.
Sitting at the feet of Jesus,
I would look upon the past;
For His love has been so gracious,
It has won my heart at last.

Sitting at the feet of Jesus,
Where can mortal be more blest?
There I lay my sins and sorrows
And, when weary, find sweet rest.
Sitting at the feet of Jesus,
There I love to weep and pray,
While I from His fullness gather
Grace and comfort ev'ry day.

Bless me, O my Saviour, bless me,
As I sit low at Thy feet.
Oh, look down in love upon me;
Let me see Thy face so sweet.
Give me, Lord, the mind of Jesus;
Make me holy as He is.
May I prove I've been with Jesus,
Who is all my righteousness.

—Asa Hull

Sit quietly in His presence. Thank Him for His righteousness that has made you righteous. Let Him bless you.

MEMORY CHALLENGE

Do you look forward to seeing the Lord? Why?

DAY FOUR

Naomi and Ruth Wait

Read Ruth 3:15-18.

1. How did Boaz once again show his kindness and generosity to Naomi and Ruth?

2. How does God respond to our giving? (Refer to 2 Corinthians 9:6-11.)

3. What response comes from those whose needs have been supplied through the giving of others? (Refer to 2 Corinthians 9:12-15.)

4. Naomi once again gave Ruth good counsel. What was her advice (Ruth 3:18)?

5. God encourages us in waiting. Record phrases of instruction from the following passages:

   Psalm 27:14

   Psalm 40:1

Psalm 130:5-7

Lamentations 3:25-26

Hosea 12:2-6 (Record verse 6)

6. Name the benefits of waiting given in the following scriptures:

   Isaiah 30:18

   Isaiah 64:4

   Luke 12:35-40

7. Why would it be hard for Ruth to wait?

8. Is there something that you want immediately?

   Is it something you're impatient about?

   Have you tried working it out yourself?

   Do you want to work it out yourself?

9. How hard is it for you to wait for God to work out the circumstances?

10. Respond personally to a scripture you examined in item 5 or 6. Where you have been disobedient to God's truths, confess it to God, ask His forgiveness, and thank Him for His faithfulness to forgive you.

    Asking God for insight, how do you now need to apply these truths to your circumstances?

Now to him who is able to do immeasurably more than all we ask or imagine, according to His power that is at work within us (Ephesians 3:20). Praise God for what He is going to do in your life and circumstances while you're waiting for His perfect timing.

Believe that He will continue to work in your life to remind you of His power in circumstances when you're waiting.

MEMORY CHALLENGE

I myself will see Him with my own eyes—I, and not another. _______ _______ _________ _________

_________ _______!

Job 19:27

DAY FIVE

Boaz at the Gate

Read Ruth 4:1-12.

1. While Naomi and Ruth were waiting, where were the two men who were qualified to become Ruth's kinsman-redeemer?

All official business and civic affairs were conducted at the town gate. This would compare to a combination of city hall and county courthouse today.

2. The first response of the relative when he was given the opportunity to redeem Elimelech's property was that he would redeem it. Why did he change his mind?

Scripture does not explain why the relative could not redeem the property and marry Ruth. Here are some possibilities:

- He may have been unable to buy the land and also support Ruth and Naomi.
- Mahlon and Kilion had both died after marrying a Moabite, and he feared the same fate.
- If Ruth would have a son, he would automatically inherit all of Elimelech's property, plus a part of the redeemer's property.

3. How was the transaction legalized?

What could Ruth have done to this relative? (Refer to Deuteronomy 25:7-10.)

The transaction was completed. Boaz and Ruth could now be married. Boaz had risked losing Ruth to his relative, but he wanted his actions to be legal and in obedience to God's laws.

Ruth, whose people were enemies of Israel, had come to Bethlehem motivated by her deep love for Naomi and Naomi's God. She had placed herself at the mercy of a wealthy Israelite, a near-kinsman of her mother-in-law.

Boaz had watched Ruth through the harvest seasons. He had seen her work, heard her talk, and knew her heart's desire during the daring and uncertain time she waited at the threshing floor. The heart of Boaz had been moved to shelter her under the spreading wings of his own name and inheritance. He had purchased Ruth for himself, before all the assembled elders and people, to bring forth a heritage through her, although their first child would become the heir of Elimelech and his sons.

Boaz took upon himself a joyous task in planning to marry Ruth. But he risked all the losses the unnamed kinsman feared. He accepted large responsibilities. He took on the responsibility of Naomi as well as Ruth. He promised to bring up a child for his dead kinsman.

4. As the elders and all those at the gate gave their blessings, they gave special recognition to those whom they wanted Ruth to be like. Who were they?

Rachel and Leah were the wives of Jacob, the father of the 12 tribes of Israel. Rachel's sons were Joseph and Benjamin. The sons of Rachel's maid were Dan and Naphtali. Leah's sons were Reuben, Simeon, Levi, Judah, Issachar, and Zebulun, plus one daughter, Dinah. The sons of Leah's maid were Gad and Asher.

> The greatest blessing for an Israelite woman was to bear many children. Rachel bore only two, but her husband loved her dearly. Leah bore six sons and one daughter. Both women became ancestors of Israel. . . . Even though she [Ruth] was a Moabitess, they hoped for her all that came to Israelite women.[1]

The elders also prayed that Ruth might be famous in Bethlehem. That prayer was answered when Ruth's great-grandson David was born in Bethlehem as the shepherd king and a great type of the heavenly King Jesus, who himself was born in the same place 1,300 years later. It was a prophetic prayer.

The persistence with which Boaz sought out the nearest of kin in order to gain the right to marry Ruth discloses not only some interesting customs but also the depth of his love for Ruth. This is one of the greatest love stories of all times.

MEMORY CHALLENGE

Write Job 19:27 from memory.

DAY SIX

The Ancestry of Messiah

Read Ruth 4:13-22.

1. The first day Ruth gleaned in the fields of Boaz, he prayed a blessing over her (Ruth 2:12). How had Boaz answered his own prayer for Ruth?

With the birth of Obed, we see the pendulum swing toward joy for Ruth and Naomi. As widows, they had been suffering in Moab and since their return to Bethlehem.

2. These closing verses in the Book of Ruth focus on Naomi. How do you see the contrast between Naomi's earlier condition and now, at the time of Obed's birth?

   Ruth 1:19-21

   Ruth 4:14-16

3. What do the women think of Ruth?

Ruth's love for her mother-in-law was well known by Naomi's friends as well as throughout Bethlehem. From chapter 1 to the end of the Book of Ruth, we have seen Ruth's consistent kindness toward others. Kindness is a quality shown in every chapter of Ruth: Naomi's kindness to her daughters-in-law, Ruth's kindness to Naomi, and Boaz's kindness to Ruth and Naomi.

Ruth had been drawn to the God of the Israelites through their love and kindness to her. "In Ruth's case the moment of moral choice in showing *hesed* [God's love and faithfulness] to Naomi was the moment of her conversion, when she made Naomi's God her God, though no doubt the conviction had been forming within her that Yahweh was the loving God, whom she desired above all else. . . . How attractive it becomes to others when God's people reflect His faithful love to them in their dealings with one another!"[1]

4. Why should we be kind to one another?

   Ephesians 4:32

   From Ruth 2:10-12, in your own words, explain Boaz's reason for being kind to Ruth.

Kindness keeps on being passed from one person to another until it returns to you.

5. Where do Christians get kindness? Refer to Galatians 5:22.

Kindness is a spontaneous work of the Holy Spirit within us.

6. Read John 15:4-8. Record verse 4.

7. What are some blessings from kindness? Record the first phrase from each of the following verses (from *The Living Bible* if available).

   Proverbs 11:16

   Proverbs 11:17

8. From Titus 3:3-7, in your own words, explain what the greatest kindness of all means to you today.

9. Record the genealogy of David from Boaz. (Refer to Matthew 1:5-6.)

The story of Ruth introduces us to David. It gives background for certain incidents and attitudes in his life. David apparently was aware of his Moabitish ancestry. When in trouble with Saul, David asked protection for his father and mother from the king of Moab. They stayed with the king of Moab as long as David was in distress (1 Samuel 22:3-4).

In spiritual perception, the Book of Ruth stands at the doorway to the Gospel. It demonstrates God's openness to people of a country other than Israel, and shows the kindness of God's gracious plans for those whom He chooses, and who choose to follow Him.[2]

God had promised Adam and Eve a "seed" that would conquer Satan (Genesis 3:15, KJV). The Old Testament is the revealing of that promised "seed," Jesus Christ. The coming Messiah was from the line of Adam and Eve through their son Seth on through Noah and his son Shem until Abraham (Genesis 5; 11:10-26). God promised Abraham that through him all the families of the earth would be blessed, a promise that the "seed" would come through Abraham's descendants (Genesis 12:1-3, the Abrahamic covenant). God reaffirmed this covenant with Isaac and Jacob (Genesis 26:1-4; 28:10-14). Then Judah, one of Jacob's twelve sons, was promised the royal line, the line of Christ (Genesis 49:10). In 2 Samuel 7:12-13 God promised David that his descendant would reign forever. The Messiah would come through the line of David. Ruth is the book that traces the line of Judah to David, the lineage of the Messiah. It is crucial to the Old Testament purpose of presenting the ancestry of Christ.

The Moabitish ancestry of Ruth became part of the human ancestry of our Lord. Ruth was one of only four women mentioned in the genealogy of Christ. Of these, Tamar gave birth through an illicit relationship with her father-in-law. Rahab made her living as a harlot. Bathsheba conceived out of wedlock. Ruth alone was unstained in character, but she came of Gentile blood. The Book of Ruth takes us back to our spiritual roots and reminds us that God's ways are always high and creative, and graciously full of love.[3]

The study of the ancestry of Messiah is of no true value to us unless we have accepted Him as Messiah. If there is the slightest doubt in your heart, as you consider your relationship with the Lord, prayerfully read Psalm 139:23-24—*Search me, O God, and know my heart; test me and know my anxious thoughts. See if there is any offensive way in me, and lead me in the way everlasting.*

MEMORY CHALLENGE

Review Job 19:25 and 27. Quote these verses from memory.

Notes

Introduction to Jonah

1. Armor D. Peisker, "Jonah," *Beacon Bible Commentary* (Kansas City: Beacon Hill Press of Kansas City, 1966), 161.

Jonah—Lesson 1, Day 2

1. Lloyd John Ogilvie, *Lord of the Impossible* (Nashville: Abingdon Press, 1984), 178.

Jonah—Lesson 1, Day 4

1. R. G. Lee, *A Guide to Christian Workers* (Memphis: Thomas Nelson Publishers, 1978), 1285.

Jonah—Lesson 1, Day 6

1. John G. Butler, *Jonah* (Clinton, Iowa: LBC Publications, 1994), 131.
2. Ibid., 132.

Jonah—Lesson 2, Day 5

1. Warren W. Wiersbe, *Chapter by Chapter Bible Commentary* (Nashville: Thomas Nelson Publishers), 592.

Jonah—Lesson 2, Day 6

1. E. P. Pusey, *The Minor Prophets* (Grand Rapids: Baker Book House, 1963), 423; quoted in *Beacon Bible Commentary* (Kansas City: Beacon Hill Press of Kansas City, 1966), 184.

Esther—Lesson 1, Day 1

1. Clarence Edward Macartney, *Great Women of the Bible* (Grand Rapids: Kregel Publications, 1992), 22-23.

Esther—Lesson 1, Day 4

1. Ray Stedman, *A Pair of Queens*, PBC Homepage (Discovery Publishing, Ray Stedman Library, 1995), <pbc.org/dp/stedman/esther/o\0032.html>.

Esther—Lesson 1, Day 5

1. G. Campbell Morgan, *An Exposition of the Whole Bible* (Westwood, N.J.: Fleming H. Revell Company, 1959), 197.

Esther—Lesson 2, Day 1

1. Beth Moore, *Praying God's Word* (Nashville: Broadman and Holman Publishers, 2000), 89-90.

Esther—Lesson 2, Day 3

1. Edith Dean, *All of the Women of the Bible* (Memphis: Castle Books, 1998), 148.

Esther—Lesson 2, Day 4

1. Dan R. Crawford, *A Night of Tragedy* (Colorado Springs: Baker Books, 2000), 68-69.

Esther—Lesson 2, Days 5 & 6

1. "Persecution: A Brief History," *The Voice of the Martyrs* Newsletter, December 1999, 10-11. (P.O. Box 443, Bartlesville, OK 74005-0443; 800-747-0085; <www.persecution.com>). Used by permission.

Esther—Lesson 3, Day 2

1. Ray Stedman, "Good Grief," Series on Esther, PBC Homepage (Discovery Publishing, Ray Stedman Library, 1995), <pbc.org/dp/stedman/esther/0034.html>.

Esther—Lesson 3, Day 3

1. Written by Kay Wilson, Wisdom of the Word board member, 2000.

Esther—Lesson 3, Day 4

1. Chuck Swindoll, *Esther: A Woman of Strength and Dignity* (Dallas: Word Publishing, 1997), 97.
2. Andy Anderson, *Fasting Changed My Life* (Nashville: Broadman Press, 1997), 44.

Esther—Lesson 3, Day 5

1. Gien Karssen, *Her Name Is Woman* (Colorado Springs: Navpress, 1975), 117.

Esther—Lesson 4, Day 1

1. *NIV Life Application Bible* (Wheaton, Ill.: Tyndale Publishers; and Grand Rapids: Zondervan Publishing House, 1991), 2043.

Esther—-Lesson 4, Day 3

1. Mark Roberts, *The Communicator's Commentary—Ezra, Nehemiah, Esther* (Dallas: Word Books, 1993), 398.

Esther—Lesson 4, Day 5

1. *Touch Point Bible* (Wheaton, Ill.: Tyndale Publishers, 1996), 118.

Esther—Lesson 5, Day 5

1. Swindoll, *Esther*, 97.

Ruth—Lesson 1, Day 3

1. *Matthew Henry's Commentary*, vol. 2; written 1708 (Peabody, Mass.: Hendrickson Publishers, 1991), 202.

Ruth—Lesson 2, Day 1

1. *NIV Life Application Bible* (Wheaton, Ill.: Tyndale Publishers; and Grand Rapids: Zondervan Publishing Company, 1991), 426.

Ruth—Lesson 2, Day 3

1. *Wycliffe Bible Commentary* (Chicago: Moody Press, 1962), 27.

Ruth—Lesson 2, Day 5

1. Margaret Hess, *Love Knows No Barriers* (Wheaton, Ill.: Victor Books, 1979), 131.

Ruth—Lesson 2, Day 6

1. *The New Bible Commentary Revised* (Grand Rapids: Wm. B. Eerdmans Publishing Company, 1970; revised 1978), 278.
2. Hess, *Love Knows No Barriers*, 131.
3. Ibid.

CPSIA information can be obtained
at www.ICGtesting.com
Printed in the USA
LVHW100802130319
610437LV00007B/7/P